LESSONS
in
LEADERSHIP

25 Essential Lessons
for Godly Leaders

D1602916

LESSONS in LEADERSHIP

25 Essential Lessons for Godly Leaders

Dr. Jack Trieber

For further information write:

North Valley Publications
941 Clyde Avenue • Santa Clara, California 95054

DEDICATION

Lessons in Leadership is dedicated to my loving wife
Cindie, who for nearly 20 years has been my mate,
my friend, my cheerleader, and a godly helpmeet.

TABLE OF CONTENTS

TABLE OF CONTENTS

continued

INTRODUCTION

WHAT IS LEADERSHIP? Someone once said that leadership is providing guidance and direction. Another defined it as example. Yet another describes leadership as inspiring others. Theodore Roosevelt said, "A leader is one that can get others to do what they don't want to do and gets them to enjoy doing what they don't want to do." Defined in one word, leadership is direction.

Everybody is a leader. God has placed you in the very position in which you find yourself; therefore, you are a leader. Mothers lead and direct children; teachers lead and direct students. In the areas of medicine, education, commerce, transportation, and government, we have leaders. In the home and in the church, we have leaders. Everyone who reads this book is a leader.

There are degrees of leadership. In schools, there are leaders among the students. Many times they lead because they are bigger, older, better looking, taller, or stronger than the other students. However, leaders are not always bigger, taller, or stronger. Go to a nursery; the smallest, feistiest baby may be providing leadership there. In the average home in America today, it is not the father who leads. It is not the mother who leads. In many cases, it is the children who are leading the home. The entire home revolves around a little baby. That influential little baby says, "We're doing it this way; if you don't like it, I'm throwing a fit." When he begins to scream, the parents say, "We'll give in. We'll do it your way." We may use a different set of words as we give in, but we do give in. Perhaps we say, "All right, I'll buy you a brand new car. I know you're only seven years old, but just don't cry anymore." We give in, and our children provide the leadership for our homes.

The Bible contains two books that go hand in hand regarding leadership, Ezra and Nehemiah. Ezra was written years before Nehemiah and is a book that deals with restoration. Ezra tells about the restoration of the Temple and of Temple worship. Nehemiah is a book that deals with rebuilding and reconstruction. We will see how Nehemiah dealt with being a leader.

You do not realize how hard it is to be the leader until you find yourself in that position. For example, being a husband looks easy when you are single; when you become a husband, you realize the difficulties. Before they are married, women can tell anyone about how to be a wife; but being a good wife is a lot harder than it appears. The same is true of child rearing. I knew how to rear kids—before I had them. When I came to this church, I would preach, "Rear your kids this way"; but when I became a father, child rearing did not work as easily as I thought it would.

I can recall when I was asked to pastor North Valley Baptist Church. I was excited and thrilled about going there. I will never forget the lump in my throat and the knot in my stomach when I arrived on March 1, 1976. I thought, "What in the world have I done to these poor people? I told them I could be their pastor." Once you get a position of leadership, it is very scary.

The book of Nehemiah is exciting because it shows how to deal with government, how to deal with disgruntled people, how to deal with employees, how to organize, how to agonize, and how to get a job done. As the book of Ezra is twofold, the rebuilding of the Temple and the restoring of the worship, the book of Nehemiah is also twofold. Chapters 1 through 6 deal with the reconstruction of the wall; chapters 7 through 13 deal with re-instructing the people. The rebuilding process the Israelites followed was somewhat backwards. In the book of Ezra, they rebuilt the Temple; and for ninety years it lay open to siege from their enemies because there was no wall around their city, no wall around their Temple, and no wall around their worship. Chapters 1 through 6, therefore, deal with the rebuilding of the wall of Jerusalem.

There is a tremendous illustration here. It is great that we want to worship, but we should put some parameters around our worship and around our lives. We should say there are some things we will do and some things we will not do. Before we try to share our worship, we should first build some walls around our own lives. Teenagers would be wise to build a wall of purity around their lives and say, "This is the wall around my purity." That is what we need in our country today—for our children's sake. We need somebody to stand up and preach purity again and believe purity again. We need somebody to say, "Kids, listen. Get some walls built around your life as to what you are going to do and what you are not going to do. And if your peers say, 'Do this,' you won't do it because you have the wall of purity built around your life. You'll say, 'There are some things I can do, and there are some things I cannot do and will not do.' "

The wall of that city surrounded a population of one to two million people. It was not a little wall! It would be like building a wall around the Santa Clara Valley, which has 1.5 million residents. Nehemiah gathered the workers together and divided them into companies. Over those companies he had division leaders, and over the division leaders he had executives or other leaders. They began construction, and in fifty-two days they completed the wall. Unbelievable!

If you are going to delegate, you will have to regulate. Nehemiah was an organized man. He was able to get his leaders together and get reports back from them. The entire book of Nehemiah shows us how to do that. It is an exciting book, a thrilling book.

I trust that the Holy Spirit will convey the truth of each chapter as you read this book. It is my prayer that *Lessons in Leadership* will help us become Biblical leaders.

CHAPTER 1

PRAYER

*The words of Nehemiah the son of Hachaliah. And it came
to pass in the month Chisleu, in the twentieth year, as I was
in Shushan the palace, That Hanani, one of my brethren,
came, he and certain men of Judah; and I asked them
concerning the Jews that had escaped, which were left of the
captivity, and concerning Jerusalem. And they said unto me,
The remnant that are left of the captivity there in the province
are in great affliction and reproach: the wall of Jerusalem
also is broken down, and the gates thereof are burned with
fire. And it came to pass, when I heard these words, that I
sat down and wept, and mourned certain days, and fasted,
and prayed before the God of heaven.*

❧ Nehemiah 1:1-4

Introduction

NEHEMIAH WAS A CAPTIVE, a prisoner of war. The war had
ended, and he was being treated well. He could
have been freed, but he retained his position. In fact, he was the
king's cupbearer (Nehemiah 1:11). The king's cupbearer was one
who tasted the king's food before he ate it to be sure no one had
contaminated it, one who protected the king from eating poisoned
food. A real bond could grow between a king and his cupbearer.
In this case, a bond did grow between Nehemiah and the king.
The king began to sincerely care for Nehemiah, and Nehemiah
was concerned for the king. Every time Nehemiah would taste
something, he was offering his life for the king's life.

During the Jewish month of Chisleu (our December), Nehemiah

received a report about the deplorable condition of God's people in Jerusalem. Even though he was a prisoner of war, he was still concerned about his own people. Even though he was in a distant country, he was concerned for his fellow Jews. How it must have spoken to his heart when he heard of the Jews' affliction, and when he learned that the gates of Jerusalem had been burned. As he heard the firsthand report that his people were a reproach, that they were being scoffed and ridiculed, and that they were poverty-stricken, he became heartbroken.

Have you ever had bad news brought to you? I can recall several times when I had to tell someone that one of their loved ones had died. I said, "I'm coming over. I want to see you for a few minutes."

They would meet me at the door and say, "Pastor, what is it?"

I would say, "Can we sit down for a few minutes?"

I can recall years ago when three little girls from one of our bus routes came home from summer camp. The mom called me that morning and said that the dad had just died. I picked the girls up when the bus came in from camp, and I took them to their house. They said, "Why are you picking us up?"

I said, "I want to talk to you when we get home. Tell me all about camp." We had some small talk. When we got to the house I said, "Girls, let's all sit down here on the couch together. Your mom has something to talk to you about." They sat down, and we told them that their father had died.

It is always hard, so you sit down because your legs feel like jelly. When Nehemiah heard about his people, he sat down (Nehemiah 1:4).

After hearing the discouraging report in December, Nehemiah did not talk to the king about the situation until the Jewish month Nisan, which is our April (Nehemiah 2:1). Between the month of December when he heard the report about Jerusalem, and April when he spoke with the king, approximately four months elapsed. What was Nehemiah, this great leader and man of influence, doing for these four months? During this time, Nehemiah did four things:

first, he wept. I weep when I hear that someone has heartache or sorrow. Second, he mourned. Mourning is a deep agonizing, a grief so severe that it takes away your appetite. Third, he fasted. That is, he chose not to eat so he could commune with God more intensely. Fourth, he prayed. If we are going to be Biblical leaders, we must learn to pray. Before Nehemiah spoke with the king and before he began to lead God's people, he prayed.

A Leader Must Learn to Pray

The first principle of leadership is prayer. If you are a leader—and we are all leaders because we all provide direction to others—you need to learn how to pray. You cannot lead without prayer. Nehemiah prayed four months before he did one thing. He prayed, as we will see, day and night. For four months, day and night, he just prayed and prayed and prayed and prayed and prayed. No wonder he had such success. He started with prayer.

Remember the great preaching described in the second and third chapters of Acts, and the persecution described in Acts 4? Prior to all these events, they *"all continued in one accord in prayer"* (Acts 1:14). Before there was ever any great power in chapter 2, before there was ever any preaching in chapter 3, there was prayer in chapter 1. Before there was ever any fire coming down at Mt. Carmel (I Kings 18), Elijah bowed his knee and prayed to God on behalf of Israel. If you will follow prayer through the Bible and look at every major miracle and every major accomplishment that took place, you will always find that prayer preceded it.

A Leader Must Learn What Prayer Is

Prayer is asking.

> *Ask, and it shall be given you; seek, and ye shall find; knock, and it shall be opened unto you.*
>
>   ❧ Matthew 7:7

The Bible then speaks about a father-son relationship.

> *If ye then, being evil, know how to give good gifts unto your children, how much more shall your Father which is in heaven give good things to them that ask him?*
>
>   ❧ Matthew 7:11

One of the reasons you do not have many of the things you need is because you do not ask, for *"ye have not, because ye ask not"* (James 4:2). Nothing great can ever be accomplished for God without prayer, nothing. *"In every thing by prayer and supplication with thanksgiving"* (Philippians 4:6). Everything is to be done with prayer, everything. *"Men ought always to pray, and not to faint"* (Luke 18:1). I Thessalonians 5:17 says, *"Pray without ceasing."* Just keep at it! If you are having a hard time with victory in your life, just keep on praying.

> What a friend we have in Jesus,
> All our sins and griefs to bear!
> What a privilege to carry
> Everything to God in prayer!
> O what peace we often forfeit,
> O what needless pain we bear,
> All because we do not carry
> Everything to God in prayer!

A Leader Must Learn to Compliment God

We find the opening of Nehemiah's prayer:

> *O LORD God of heaven, the great and terrible God, that keepeth covenant and mercy for them that love him and observe his commandments: Let thine ear now be attentive.*
> ᏮNehemiah 1:5-6

Notice how he compliments God. If you will look at many of the prayers of the great prophets of God, they always compliment God first, like a wife often does with her husband. She may make him a special meal and then say, "Honey, you're a great husband!" When this happens, men, beware! Her next line may be, "Do you want to go shopping tonight?"

The husband may respond, "All right, if you want to." If he still has not caught on, he might say, "Where do you want to go?" And she will say, "Just to the store." Actually, she already has the dress in mind. She saw it there that day!

He says, "All right."

As they walk through the store, she suddenly jerks him and

says, "Look at that pretty dress!" This wife has made a lot of progress towards buying a new dress, and it started when she first complimented her husband.

The prophets complimented God. They told God He was wonderful, and there is nothing wrong with that. If we do not tell God how wonderful He is, who will? You say, "God already knows." Surely He knows. He knows everything, and sometimes I tell Him, "God, You know I'm here to compliment you for a little while, but I really do mean what I'm saying. You are great." I may then quote these verses:

> *When I consider thy heavens, the work of thy fingers, the moon and the stars, which thou hast ordained; what is man, that thou art mindful of him?*
>
>   ❧ Psalm 8:3-4

I may say, "God, you are so great!" and then begin singing "How Great Thou Art."

> O Lord my God, when I in awesome wonder
> Consider all the worlds Thy hands have made,
> I see the stars, I hear the rolling thunder,
> Thy power throughout the universe displayed!
>
> Carl Boberg. Translated by Stuart K. Hine.
> © Copyright 1953 (Renewed 1981) by MANNA
> MUSIC, INC., 35255 Brooten Road, Pacific City,
> OR 97135. International Copyright Secured. All
> Rights Reserved. Used by Permission.

After this, I may say, "Now, I've got some needs I need to talk to you about because You are great, and You can meet them." I oftentimes talk to the Lord that way. I have to. I want to remind Him what I think of Him. God pity the wife who does not compliment her husband sometimes, not necessarily just to get things from him. God pity the husband who does not compliment and encourage his wife, who does not let his wife know how great and wonderful she is. And God pity us when we do not take time to compliment Him for all He is and all He can do.

A Leader Must Learn to Pray Night and Day

*Let thine ear now be attentive, and thine eyes open, that thou mayest hear the prayer of thy servant, which I pray before thee now, **day and night.***

                 ❧ Nehemiah 1:6

For four months, Nehemiah prayed day and night. He said, as it were, "I'm not going to stop. I'm going to pray in the morning when I get up. I'm going to pray at nighttime. I'm going to pray during the nighttime. I'm not going to go to bed at times. I'm going to pray, pray, pray, pray."

Some of you have crises ahead of you. Some of you are in the midst of a crisis, some major, monumental thing. The only way you are going to get through it is by prayer. Mean business with God. Pray in the morning; pray at noon; pray in the evening.

Evening, and morning, and at noon, will I pray, and cry aloud: and he shall hear my voice.

                 ❧ Psalm 55:17

Pray at breakfast, lunch, and dinner—and not just for the food. Pray for your needs at breakfast, lunch, dinner, morning, noon, and night. Pray seven times a day. Just keep on praying throughout the day. Pray in the morning; pray at noon; pray in the evening. Nehemiah prayed day and night.

A Leader Must Learn that Prayer Brings Confession
Nehemiah confessed his sins to God.

*Hear the prayer of thy servant, which I pray before thee now, day and night, for the children of Israel thy servants, **and confess the sins of the children of Israel, which we have sinned against thee: both I and my father's house have sinned.***

                 ❧ Nehemiah 1:6

When you begin to walk with God and pray to God, He will reveal some things in your life that are not right. You will say, "Lord, as I'm praying I need to get some things settled here. I want to make some confessions to You. I want to get some things settled with Thee, God. I've not treated my wife the way I should.

I've not treated my husband the way I should. I've been short with my children. I've not read Your Book like I should. I've not prayed. I've not been a soul winner like I should. I've not been kind and pleasing to Thee and to others. God, I see it now." It is amazing the things God reveals to you when you begin to pray. That is the wonderful thing about prayer—as you pray, God reveals things to you, and you confess those things and open a channel of communication with God.

Before Nehemiah could have an open channel of communication between man and man, he had to have a channel of communication between man and God. You say, "I just have problems with people around me." Often, the reason you are having problems between man and man is because you are having problems between man and God. I dare say that if you get things straightened out between you and God, a lot of things between you and man will be straightened out, too. Before you say something negative about somebody, think, "Have I been praying?" You will never be the right kind of a leader if you have not learned to pray. Without prayer, you will lead someone; but you will lead him down the wrong path.

Pray on the airplane; pray while you are driving to the office; pray in the park; pray as you are riding the train; pray while you are in the office; pray wherever you may be. Just pray. You may not always be able to kneel. Just pray. Pray about everything. Luke 18:1 says, *"Men ought always to pray, and not to faint."* Pray about everything. Just pray. As the songwriter said, "Keep on praying till light breaks through."

Great leaders pray. Do you?

CHAPTER 2

COMPASSION

And it came to pass, when I heard these words, that I sat down and wept, and mourned certain days, and fasted, and prayed before the God of heaven.

≈ Nehemiah 1:4

Introduction
NEHEMIAH 1:4 CONTAINS four leadership principles. When Nehemiah heard of the great trouble in the city of Jerusalem, he wept, mourned, fasted, and prayed. In this chapter, we deal with *compassion.* His weeping showed he was moved with compassion and tenderness. Leaders are compassionate. If we are not careful, we will say, "I don't want to be compassionate; I'm Mr. Macho." Yet, the greater the man, the more tenderness he must possess. This does not mean he cannot have muscles or strength, or that he cannot be a man's man. It means, however, that he needs to have compassion. There tends to be a real lack of compassion on the part of each of us today. The pastor needs to have compassion. Deacons, staff members, fathers, mothers, employers, and foremen also need compassion.

Four Signs of a Compassionate Leader
The Bible says Nehemiah did four things when he heard these things. *He wept.* When he heard about the condition of his brethren, he sat down and wept. The word *wept* means to cry out of grief and a broken heart. The Jews were his people. When he heard of their condition, all his strength was taken from him. His

knees got weak, he sat down, and he wept. *He mourned.*
Mourning is an inner groaning, an aching, a tender heart on the
inside, a writhing in pain. He wept—he showed his grief on the
outside. He mourned—it was tearing him apart on the inside. *He*
fasted, that is, he did without food. And *he prayed* before the
Lord God of heaven. Nehemiah was obviously moved easily. He
saw a need in somebody else, and he was moved quickly.
Nehemiah was not hard. He did not say, "Boy, I'm the boss. I'm
the authority."

You do not always have to tell everyone about your authority.
Some husbands say to their wives, "Obey me! The Word of God
says so." When you have to constantly remind your wife that you
are the leader, you are probably not the leader, and it is probably
not her fault. I believe God's Word teaches that.

Before Nehemiah did anything, he began to be moved with
tenderness. He was not hard. This trial did not make him bitter, it
made him better. We need to learn to express feelings as Nehemiah
did. We need to be able to weep with those that weep, laugh with
those that laugh, cry with those that cry, and rejoice with those
that rejoice. Oh, how we need to learn that today!

Compassion is a leadership quality. If you are an employer,
you are not the right kind of employer if you have not learned
compassion. If you are a husband, you have not learned the joy
of being a husband unless you have learned some compassion. If
you are a wife, you have not learned the joy of being a wife unless
you have learned to have some real compassion, love, and
tenderness. Never be hard and mean.

Jesus Showed Compassion
The shortest verse in the Bible is John 11:35, *"Jesus wept."* I
do not believe the theme of that verse is accidental. It shows me
that God has some emotions. God's Son had compassion and
was moved easily. What is the context of John 11:35? Lazarus
had died. Was it the death of Lazarus that caused Jesus to weep?
No, but everybody was crying. Lazarus' sisters were crying, and
the Bible says, *"Jesus wept."* Consider this verse. The first word
is *Jesus.* It tells us Who He is and what He is—He is Jesus, the

Son of God. The second word tells us that He wept. Jesus wept; He showed emotion. There was a tenderness there. It does not say He became hard. Jesus did not say, "Get up, you guys. Lazarus went to heaven. What are you crying about?" By the way, He could have easily preached that message. He could have easily rebuked them and said, "Don't you know that Lazarus is in heaven? What's wrong with you people? I've been here pouring out My heart to you day after day, preaching to Mary and Martha, to the Jews, and to the women over there crying. I've been giving Myself to you. Now your brother died and went to heaven, the place I've been talking about, and you're just sitting here boo-hooing." Jesus did not talk like that. He knew that heaven is far better than earth; but He also knew they did not comprehend that.

Our children cannot understand many of the things that we comprehend. Sometimes we give instructions to our children and when they do not catch on we get upset. This sharply contrasts Jesus' attitude. He had taught these Jews about heaven, a better place, but they did not catch on. The only thing they seemed capable of understanding was that they had lost their brother Lazarus in death, and that Lazarus would not have died if Jesus had been there. Yet, Jesus demonstrated compassion, not impatience.

Our lack of compassion shows when men impatiently give instructions about how the home should be run, or when women become frustrated when their husbands do not seem to comprehend their input. Too often we throw up our arms in disgust and say something unkind like, "This jerk will never learn!" or "You're the meanest person in the world to live with! I just don't understand you." Then, most humiliatingly of all, especially when children and others are present, we slam the door and tear it off the hinges. We do things like this because we lack compassion.

Shopping is one of the things that most men dislike. I was talking with Brother Romkee, one of my church members, and I said, "Brother Romkee, I'm sorry that you have to give so much of your time, and that you're here working every night on the building. God bless you."

"Thank you, Pastor," he said. "It sure beats shopping!" I agree! However, compassion would lead a husband to go shopping with his wife if she wants his company.

Sunday morning is an excellent time for men to have compassion. Most Sunday mornings the husband is in the car waiting for the wife, and he is getting more upset and more upset and more upset and more upset. So, he does the thing he should not do—he honks the horn! His wife says to herself, "Just for that, I'm going to be another minute."

She finally comes out. While she is getting in the car, he is jerking the car out of the driveway while her door is still open. All the way to church, he drives like Parnelli Jones, going through yellow lights and almost red lights. He is all upset. To the children in the back seat, he says, "Sit down. You sit down now!" His wife is over there, and what is she doing? She is polishing her nails, thereby stinking up the car, and making it impossible for the husband to breathe. He cannot breathe, so he rolls down the window, and she says, "My hair!"

He says, "Well, it looks better now than when you got in the car!" They come screeching to a halt in front of the church and he says, "Have a good day in Sunday school, kids." How about having a little compassion!

Bible Characters Showed Compassion

Ecclesiastes 3:4 says there is *"A time to weep."* In John 11:31, we read that Mary wept after the death of Lazarus; she was moved with compassion. In I Samuel 1, Hannah sat down and wept because she had no child. Read Ruth 1:9, *"And they lifted up their voice, and wept."* David wept for his child. David wept over his sin. Jesus wept over Jerusalem. The prophets were moved with compassion. When Peter denied the Lord Jesus Christ, he went out and wept. *As I find compassionate people in the Bible, they were weeping on the behalf of someone else. God does not want us just weeping for ourselves.*

I think we need to take inventory. We should ask ourselves, "Are the tears I shed because people misunderstand me, because people don't like me, because I'm having a hard time struggling with bills, or because life is so tough? Am I weeping over me, or are my tears over other people? Are my tears over a little boy who doesn't have a father, or a little girl who doesn't have a mother, or the little children who have parents in jails? Is my weeping over families that are having a hard time? Is my weeping for joy because someone got a new car? Is my weeping for joy because someone's son or daughter turned out right for God? Am I weeping because someone's son or daughter has broken his parents' hearts?" Too often, we are weeping for ourselves.

Everyone Needs Compassion

Nehemiah was not weeping for himself, he was weeping for his people. He had compassion for them. Every child needs time every day to sit on his father's or mother's knee, time to just sit with his parents and be loved and squeezed. Children need this every day, not just once a week. Compassion is needed daily. There needs to be kissing of the children and a good-bye when they walk out the door. Compassion. The last thing a man ought to do as he leaves home for work is to hug his wife and say, "Honey, I love you." Compassion. Our teenagers need love and tenderness so much today. So often we just look at teenagers and think they are rotten kids. They need compassion. If teenagers knew one person in this world really loved them, I believe they could turn out right. Notice what it says in Romans 12:14, *"Bless them which persecute you: bless, and curse not. Rejoice with them that do rejoice, and weep with them that weep."* Compassion. We tease about mothers-in-law. However, what you need toward your mother-in-law is compassion. You need compassion toward your father-in-law, your neighbor, your employer, your employees, and toward everybody with whom you come in contact. Compassion.

Great leaders possess compassion. Do you?

CHAPTER 3

LISTENING

Hanani, one of my brethren, came, he and certain men of Judah; and I asked them concerning the Jews that had escaped, which were left of the captivity, and concerning Jerusalem. And they said unto me, The remnant that are left of the captivity there in the province are in great affliction and reproach: the wall of Jerusalem also is broken down, and the gates thereof are burned with fire.

&⋙ Nehemiah 1:2-3

Introduction

T HE THIRD PRINCIPLE OF LEADERSHIP is *listening.* This is the one that makes the difference between success and failure. It is the one, so to speak, that separates the men from the boys. This is the critical ingredient. Parents who do not learn to listen are guaranteed to fail. Employers who do not know how to listen lead businesses into failure. Each employee, mate, pastor, and church member must possess this ingredient. Without this quality, each will fail.

If a poll were taken, I estimate we would find that ninety-five to ninety-nine percent of people just do not listen. When I preach, many of my regular members do not hear what I have to say—regardless of what I do. If I stand on my head and tell funny stories the whole time, it might keep the interest of some who are here for the first time, but most people do not listen. A wife may be trying to communicate by her expressions, by her words, by her actions, or by her behavior in the home. She may not come out and say, "Look, I'm miserable in this marriage!" But, too often, she is trying to communicate something to a husband who is not listening. Many husbands do not listen.

As a pastor, I cannot tell you how many times a lady has come into my office and said, "I just was not listening. Now, I have put it all together. He had been telling me, showing me, and living that for years. Now that I have lost him, I understand what he was saying." Sadly, many wives do not listen.

If Hanani had brought his message to me instead of Nehemiah, I would have had great difficulty believing the intensity of the tragedy. I might have interrupted him before he had a chance to finish so I could announce an immediate plan of action, but Hanani had a lengthy and discouraging message. He was not merely saying they were in captivity. He was also saying, *"Jerusalem also is broken down, and the gates thereof are burned with fire"* (Nehemiah 1:3). He was saying that they were in reproach. They were being afflicted, and people were making fun of them. Physically, their people were weary and defeated; their health was broken. There was no military, so their city was completely defenseless. In addition to that, the walls were burned; materials were gone. Jerusalem was a waste. This was a long story, but **Nehemiah listened!** If you want to be a leader, you have to learn to listen.

Prayer

First, listening is developed by praying. Psalm 34:4 says, *"I sought the Lord, and he heard me."* God listens to us. The Psalmist goes on to say in verse 6, *"This poor man cried, and the Lord heard him."* Psalm 40:1 says, *"I waited patiently for the Lord; and he inclined unto me, and heard my cry."* Psalm 77:1 says, *"I cried unto God with my voice, even unto God with my voice; and he gave ear unto me."*

When we get into trouble and distress and heartache, when we have a decision to make, when we are backed up against the wall and we cry unto the Lord, we expect God to hear us. On Saturday evenings the men of our church meet for prayer. We do not kneel in the church auditorium just to bounce prayers off a ceiling. I knelt this morning and prayed to a God in heaven, and I expected Him to hear me. It would be very disillusioning and depressing if God did not hear me when I went to prayer.

Now, let's turn the situation around. When people come into our presence to speak with us, they expect us to listen. Nehemiah developed the quality of listening by praying night and day for four months. I find that the more spiritual, godly, and holy a person is and the more time he spends with God, the more he will be willing to listen. God's Word says, *"He heareth the cry of the afflicted"* (Job 34:28); and people who spend time with God seem to develop some of His qualities.

Example

Second, we learn to listen by example. I Peter 2:21 says that we are to follow in His steps, to emulate Christ in our lives. We are to be followers of Christ. He was willing to listen; and if I spend time with Him in prayer and meditation day and night, I am going to become like the Master. Therefore, if I become like Jesus, I will be more prone to listen to my children and to the other people who are part of my life. How careful we ought to be about listening! We learn by example, and the best example we have is Jesus Christ, God Almighty.

Practice

Third, we learn to listen by practice. We have to practice listening. Probably in every appointment I have with people I actually say to myself, "Are you listening to what they are saying?" We are told that we can speak about 100 words a minute, and we can hear 400 words a minute. But here is a real danger: we can think ten times faster than we can hear. That is, we can think about 4,000 words per minute.

Andy Condict is a fine musician in our church. Suppose he and I are carrying on a conversation, and he is using up his 100 words in the minute we are together. As he is speaking, I give him partial attention, but my mind also considers my next appointment, my last appointment, a building project, the church finances, the church staff, my wife, my children, and a forthcoming church service. If I only listen to him that well, I will miss much or all of what he tells me.

In appointments, this is what I constantly ask myself, "Am I thinking about what they're saying?" I have to work at that all the time.

Character

Fourth, we develop the ability to listen by having character. Hear the entire conversation. Most people allow a person to finish just a portion of the conversation and then react. Don't react. Don't jump in when somebody is speaking. Listen. Listening comes from having character. It comes from saying, "My opinion is not the important thing. What you are telling me is the important thing." Get the whole picture. Get the whole story. Hear everything before you begin to talk. Let the speaker finish his story. Nehemiah could have cut Hanani short, but he listened to the whole story instead.

Whenever you have a conversation with someone, even if it is a heated one, you ought to always show respect and never interrupt. Let the other person say what is on his heart, and then say, "All right, I've heard you speak. Now let me speak." When he begins to interrupt, just stop and say, "Wait a minute. I showed respect to you when you were talking. I did not interrupt. Now you show respect to me and let me finish."

Repetition

Fifth, you develop the ability to listen by repeating what you have heard. If you are an employer, have the employee repeat back to you what you said. Some say God gave us two ears and one mouth because He wants us to give listening a higher priority than speaking. Open your ears and close your mouth, and you will be better off for it. Wives, listen to your husbands. Husbands, listen to your wives. Parents, listen to your children.

Great leaders listen. Do you?

CHAPTER 4

FAITHFULNESS

O Lord, I beseech thee, let now thine ear be attentive to the prayer of thy servant, and to the prayer of thy servants, who desire to fear thy name: and prosper, I pray thee, thy servant this day, and grant him mercy in the sight of this man. For I was the king's cupbearer.

                             ➷ Nehemiah 1:11

Introduction

THE FOURTH QUALITY OF LEADERSHIP is *faithfulness.* To be faithful means to be reliable and dependable. Have you ever been to Yellowstone Park to see Old Faithful? It is called Old Faithful because it is always on time. It is always dependable. It is always reliable. You can count on it. Every 59 minutes Old Faithful spews forth itself. You can depend on it. That is faithfulness.

Some leaders arrive at a position of leadership and think they no longer need to be faithful. They think the people beneath them need to be faithful, but they themselves do not need to be faithful. This is one of the biggest breakdowns in leadership today. A pastor gets to a certain point, and he demands faithfulness from his people without demanding it of himself. We see it all across America today. We see it in the news media today about preachers.

By the way, the same thing is happening in homes. We demand our kids to be reliable and dependable. We say, "You left your skates out. You left your bike out. You are undependable." However, these same children sometimes watch parents become unfaithful to church, tithing, and soul winning.

In business there is a breakdown of faithfulness. Employers across America are so upset that they seem ready to pull their hair out because they have unfaithful employees. Scores of employers know what I am talking about. They want to be able to count on their workers, but so many employees are calling in sick when they are not.

Nehemiah was written about the year 446 B.C. The children of Israel went into captivity in 586 B.C. We are not told how old Nehemiah was when he became a cupbearer, but certainly he was a grown man when he began to take a leadership position in the book of Nehemiah. A cupbearer started young in life and stayed with the king because the king could not be changing cupbearers constantly. The cupbearer assured the safety of the king by tasting the king's drinks and the king's food to be sure nothing was poisoned. The king would not change his cupbearer each week because he needed to be able to depend on him. Cupbearers were appointed for life, and Nehemiah was a cupbearer. I do not know how long he had been the king's cupbearer and I cannot cite specific dates; but certainly Ezra had been in the land over twelve years, and Ezra and Nehemiah had known one another in captivity. Ezra went back to rebuild the temple, and Nehemiah went back to rebuild the walls around the city. Apparently he was a cupbearer for a long time. He was faithful.

Nehemiah's Freedom

First, Nehemiah was faithful though he was free to move. Nehemiah was born into captivity, but he did not have to stay in captivity. Ezra led the first deportation, and many of the Jews went with him. From the first deportation to Nehemiah's day, people were free to leave to go back to their homeland if they so desired. Thus, Nehemiah was free to go back to his homeland if he wanted to go.

There is a wonderful truth here: Nehemiah stayed in a position although he had the freedom to leave it. I have often wondered what binds my members to our church. No judge ever said to an area resident, "You have to attend North Valley Baptist Church."

In our grandfathers' day and age, folks tended to live in the same general area. Basically, they lived on a farm. When the son got married, he would build a house on his father's property. We are living in a day and age in which our families are scattered all over the country. I would like to see many of our families just rear their children with one church and one pastor. My wife had one pastor all of her life, and now I am her second pastor. She had her father as her pastor, and now her husband is her pastor. My father-in-law has pastored the same church for thirty-seven years. A lot of the men on his staff he held as babies over thirty years ago and dedicated them to the Lord. Now they are on his staff serving the Lord.

If we are going to build a church, a home, or a business, people are going to need to learn to be faithful, dependable, and reliable to that church, to that home, and to that business, not always moving around. We should not always be skipping from job to job.

Nehemiah's Repetition

Second, he was faithful though he performed the same task every day. When you go to work every day, it is not necessarily enjoyable. There are some days when you do not want to be there. Don't quit on that day. Being a cupbearer must certainly have bored Nehemiah at times. However, he remained faithful to a boring position.

Nehemiah's Stature

Third, Nehemiah was faithful although his position as a cupbearer could be considered insignificant. If someone asked about the nature of his job, he might have said, "I taste the king's food." That is nothing! There is no dignity in that. He was not president of a corporation or a political big shot. He ate and drank food. Though his job could be considered insignificant, he was faithful day after day.

Anyone can be faithful to a high position for a period of time, but character requires being faithful to a low position. Anyone can be faithful to sing a solo part in the choir, but you should first be faithful as a member of the choir. In Luke 16:10 we read, *"He that is faithful in that which is least is faithful also in much: and he that is unjust in the least is unjust also in much."*

If you are not faithful to the lowly, you will not be faithful to the lofty. How many times in churches across America do we hear, "This man would be a good deacon. He doesn't come to church regularly, but he's a good man. I think if he got on the deacon board he could become a good deacon." That is crazy. You do not promote a person to a position of authority to make him faithful; you promote him because he has been faithful, dependable, and reliable.

Examples of Faithfulness

Daniel 6:4 says that Daniel was found faithful. Hebrews 3:5 says Moses was found faithful. In I Corinthians 4:17, we find that Timothy was found faithful. In I Corinthians 10:13, we read, *"God is faithful."* Colossians 1:2 says, *"To the...faithful brethren."* Colossians 1:7 says, *"Epaphras...a faithful minister of Christ."* Colossians 4:7 says, *"Tychicus...a faithful minister."* In Colossians 4:9 we read about *"Onesimus, a faithful and beloved brother."* I Peter 5:12 tells of *"Sylvanus, a faithful brother."* All these people are great heroes of the faith in the Bible, but all of them had one thing in common: they were faithful, dependable, and reliable. You could count on them. The Bible says, *"Be thou faithful unto death, and I will give thee a crown of life"* (Revelation 2:10).

In our marriages, we need to be faithful until death do us part. That is how couples in our church like the Bowens and the Josts have been married for over 50 years. It has not always been rosy for them. It has not always been nice. It has not always been easy. They have not always had money. They lived through the depression, but they have learned to be faithful unto death.

We should be faithful to our church, to our Lord, to the Word of God, to tithing, to soul winning, to our mates, to our children, and to our employers. Be faithful!

Great leaders are faithful. Are you?

CHAPTER 5

LONELINESS

So I came to Jerusalem, and was there three days. And I arose in the night, I and some few men with me; neither told I any man what my God had put in my heart to do at Jerusalem: neither was there any beast with me, save the beast that I rode upon.

&⁓ Nehemiah 2:11-12

Introduction

THE FIFTH INGREDIENT OF LEADERSHIP is *loneliness*. Nehemiah was lonely. When he went to analyze the situation in Jerusalem, he only had *"some few men"* with him. He faced the loneliness of carrying his burden in silence. *"Neither told I any man what my God had put in my heart"* (Nehemiah 2:12).

> *And the rulers knew not whither I went, or what I did; neither had I as yet told it to the Jews, nor to the priests, nor to the nobles, nor to the rulers, nor to the rest that did the work.*

&⁓ Nehemiah 2:16

When Nehemiah had received permission to visit Jerusalem, the king asked how long he would be gone (Nehemiah 2:6-8). King Artaxerxes was saying, in so many words, "I want you back." If Nehemiah had not had some tremendous qualities, the king would not have been interested in his return. He might have said, "No problem. We want you to leave. Just go ahead."

It is an honor and privilege when your employer wants you to stay. You ought to work so your boss would say, "Look, I'll give you more money. What can I do to make it more attractive so you will stay?" People ought to want you to stay at the job you are now doing.

Nehemiah set a time for his return, and he went on to Jerusalem. He was the man who had indicated that he wanted to rebuild Jerusalem (Nehemiah 2:5); but before he arrived, he faced the loneliness of opposition.

> *When Sanballat the Horonite, and Tobiah the servant, the Ammonite, heard of it, it grieved them exceedingly that there was come a man to seek the welfare of the children of Israel.*
>
> ❧ Nehemiah 2:10

What a tremendous thought! It grieved these heathen that a man was coming to help the children of God.

When Nehemiah arrived in Jerusalem, he *"arose in the night"* with *"some few men"* (Nehemiah 2:11). This passage illustrates a principle I practice now that I learned from reading both secular and Christian authors. It is a good idea to keep your staff lean. Whatever business you are in, you want to keep your staff lean.

During the night, Nehemiah analyzed the problems of the city.

> *And I went out by night by the gate of the valley, even before the dragon well, and to the dung port, and viewed the walls of Jerusalem, which were broken down, and the gates thereof were consumed with fire.*
>
> ❧ Nehemiah 2:13

Notice that Nehemiah *"viewed."* Too many of us are quick to jump to action; but Nehemiah examined and analyzed his situation. Businessmen, parents, and pastors ought to always be analyzing their businesses, ministries, and homes.

The Bible makes it clear that Nehemiah did his work *"in the night"* (Nehemiah 2:15). He *"arose in the night"* (Nehemiah 2:12), and he *"went out by night"* (Nehemiah 2:13). If you are a leader, you are not going to get the job done by lying in bed watching television. Leaders know the loneliness of working through the night.

A Leader Carries Burdens for Others

A leader carries the burdens of others that he cannot share with others. When I go home at night, I deliberately do not mention anything negative about my staff. My staff, as I am, is imperfect. I know some things about the staff that I do not want my wife to know because I want her to think that the staff is perfect and flawless. When we talk about the staff, I try to lead the conversation and always say something that is good and positive. A leader can carry the burdens of others, but he cannot share that burden with others.

Though it is difficult, a leader must learn to remain silent on many things that he knows. That is one of the most difficult things I face in the ministry. People come to share their burdens and heartaches with me, and we pray together. Soon, the problems pile up, and I would like to tell somebody.

Every week pastors call me, not because I am so smart or so well educated, in fact, most pastors are probably smarter and better educated than I; but, they call because God has, for some reason, blessed our church. Consequently, many pastors look to this church for leadership. They say, "May I come to your motel room, meet with you for a while, and talk to you?"

When a pastor comes, he may be discouraged about the offerings, about the attendance, about the deacon board, about his family, or about paying his bills. When he comes to talk with me, he expects me to keep his problems in confidence.

A pastor was here last week or the week before, and we met for about three hours. I normally do not meet that long, but he was very despondent and ready to leave his church. He is a good man, but things were not going well. I did not have any idea of how to help him as he was talking. I did not know how to solve the problem. I kept asking the Lord to give me wisdom. I didn't know how to solve the problem. The pastor would talk, and I would write down notes. After about two and a half hours of this, it clicked with me what he had been doing. When I outlined for him what he had done, it was as though someone had turned on a light for him. He was thrilled. I would love to share with everyone the details of our meeting, but a leader carries burdens of others that he cannot share with others.

A Leader Carries Burdens of His Own

A leader carries burdens of his own that he cannot share with others. A leader does not have the opportunity to share his sorrow and disappointment. A leader does not have as much heartache, sorrow, and disappointment as his followers—he has more. Parents, you have more disappointment and heartache than your children. You carry a heavier load than they do. Employers, you carry a heavier load than your employees. Your pastor carries a heavier load than you do. But leaders do not have the right to share those heartaches and pressures.

Sometimes, I feel like I am going to burst. I would like to tell somebody all that I feel. I would like to tell my wife, but in doing so I must be careful not to ruin her attitude towards the ministry. I do not want her to think that the ministry is just a bunch of problems, which, by the way, is a lot of what it is because the ministry deals with people who have heartaches.

Sometimes, I would like to announce that I've got a problem, too; but I forfeited that right by being a leader. When I counsel with people who have problems smaller than mine, I sometimes want to say, "Brother, that's nothing! You want to hear about a problem? Let me tell you about mine! I am carrying a problem so big that your problem seems to be nothing!" But his little pebble is a rock to him, and I cannot help him if I take my rock and place it on top of his shoulders when he is struggling with his pebble. My duty is to take his pebble and lift it. When a man shares his burdens and heartaches, he has forfeited the right of being a leader. A leader must learn to live a lonely life. He cannot share his burdens. He cannot share his heartaches. He cannot share his disappointments. He cannot share his discouragements with others. A leader cannot do that. If he does, he forfeits the right of leadership.

If my church members walked in on a Sunday morning, and I said, "Folks, it's going to be a good day today. I'm down. I'm depressed and discouraged. Let me tell you about some of the things that have happened to me this week. It's been a bad week. I wish it were a good week, but it's just been an awful week. I've received all this hate mail, and so many bad things went on. I don't have any money, my wife is mad at me, and my kids are disobedient—but I think it's going to be a good day today."

You would say, "I don't want to listen to that guy. His wife hates him, his kids hate him, he can't pay his bills, and he's defeated. I don't want to listen to him."

There are burdens leaders cannot share with their followers. In the parent-child relationship, the children are the followers. Parents must realize that they do not have the right to say to their children, "I'm pressured now, kids. I can't take much more than this. Now, look. This is wrong; that is wrong. I just can't handle it. Stop it! Get out!"

Parents should never do things like that because children were not created to carry parents' burdens. Parents were created to carry children's burdens. Kids live under enormous pressure today because parents put pressure on them. Parents are constantly pressuring their children by complaining that they have no money. I do not think your children ought to think you have a lot of money; I think your kids ought to always think that you are just barely making it by. But consider what may happen to the child who grows up with a mom and dad who have always said, "We have no money, no money, no money. It costs too much. No, no, no." The first thing that child will do when he leaves home is try to make money. He may start living for money and destroy his life. Parents, by the very position of being parents, you have lost the right to share your burdens with your followers. A leadership position is a lonely position.

Where could I go, O where could I go;
Seeking a refuge for my soul?
Needing a friend to help me in the end,
Where could I go but to the Lord?
    J. B. Coats
    © 1940 by Stamps-Baxter, Co. in *Golden Key*

I can go to the Lord. Another songwriter wrote,

Are you weary? are you heavyhearted?
Tell it to Jesus.

Jesus was lonely. The Bible says, *"He came unto his own, and his own received him not"* (John 1:11). Alone He prayed in Gethsemane. Even His disciples fell asleep. He was alone in the mountains, alone during the nighttime. He prayed alone in the morning. All forsook Him and fled. He was alone at His trial and alone on the cross. When you become a leader, you start to live a lonely life.

Great leaders are lonely. Are you?

CHAPTER 6

EVALUATE

And I went out by night by the gate of the valley, even before the dragon well, and to the dung port, and viewed the walls of Jerusalem, which were broken down, and the gates thereof were consumed with fire. Then I went on to the gate of the fountain, and to the king's pool...Then went I up in the night by the brook, and viewed the wall, and turned back, and entered by the gate of the valley, and so returned.

ᐔ Nehemiah 2:13-15

Introduction
I F YOU ARE GOING to be a leader, you must learn to *evaluate,* or analyze, a situation. Nehemiah sat down, and he viewed the walls. He analyzed. He evaluated. He did not talk with anyone; he was just looking and examining.

Luke 14:28 says, *"For which of you, intending to build a tower, sitteth not down first, and counteth the cost, whether he have sufficient to finish it?"* That verse teaches that if a man is going to build a tower he should first sit down and evaluate; he must analyze. He should ask, "Can I finish the project?" This is exactly what Nehemiah was doing when he viewed the walls.

Evaluate Your Home
The home should be evaluated. You should take some time, a few moments daily, and perhaps some time every week and every month, to evaluate and analyze your home.

- How was my time with my children this past week?
- Was I short with them?
- Did I give them some time?
- Did I fly a kite with them?
- Did I throw a baseball with my children this past week?
- Did we play hide-and-seek?
- Did we have fun as a family?
- Did we pop corn together?
- Did we take a ride?

Evaluate your home. Do you live from crisis to crisis? Stop it. For example, if you evaluate and find that you are far in debt, get yourself on a plan. Figure it out. Perhaps you will say, "It's going to be three years of biting the bullet, and then we'll be out of debt."

Be sure to include your wife in your evaluation, not just your children.

- How was my time with my wife this past week?
- When was the last time I bought my wife a dress?
- When was the last time I gave her a bonus for the groceries?
- When was the last time I told her I loved her?
- When was the last time I wrote her a note and told her she was the greatest thing that ever happened to my life?
- Did I do something for my wife that was special?
- Did I express my love for her every day?

No wonder some men have problems with their wives. They treat them like dirt. No wonder some husbands do not like their wives. They are treated like scum. Analyze! What type of husband are you? What type of wife are you? What type of parent are you?

Analyze the direction of your home. Where will your home be at the present rate of what you are doing right now? Consider these questions:

- If I keep doing what I'm doing, am I going to lose my husband?

- If I keep doing what I am doing right now, am I going to lose my wife?
- If I keep doing what I'm doing, will my teenagers listen to me, since they are not listening to me while they are now in grade school?

Analyze and evaluate your home.

Evaluate Your Fun

Do you have fun with your family? You might say, "Well, two years ago we went to Disneyland." Friend, that doesn't count. Your kids have lived more than 700 days since two years ago. I am not saying that every day has to be a party, but you could almost make it a party at night. Try popcorn, ice cream, wrestling, taking a ride, having family devotions, flying a kite, or playing basketball. Analyze your family fun.

Evaluate Your Business

The same is true in business today. A business leader must take the time to evaluate. You need to analyze statistics:

- What did our income do this quarter compared to last quarter in the business?
- What did it do this quarter compared to last year at this quarter?
- What did it do last month?
- What did it do last week?
- What did we do in volume today?
- Are we overstaffed? Do we, as most places, have too many employees around here?

Where are you right now?

Where is your business today? How did you get where you are? For example, if you are in debt, that is where you are; but consider how you got where you are. How did you get in debt? How did this happen? Things do not just happen. We make them happen.

Analyze how you got in debt. Was it American Express, Master

Card, or Visa that began to control your life? By the way, I would take careful consideration to find out if there is a particular time each month that you start charging more than any other time of the month.

Where are you going?

At the present rate of what you are doing now, where will your business be five years from now?

How do you plan to get there?

You must have a method of reaching your goal. For example, when people say they will rear some godly kids, I often ask how they plan to get there. By hocus-pocus? It does not work that way. Evaluate. Analyze.

The Bible says Nehemiah viewed the walls. He analyzed. If you are going to sit down and build a tower, you should take the time to examine what you are going to do. Most of our Christian homes today are too busy. We get up Monday morning and rush to school or to work; we rush home and rush to do something else. We are busy all day long, and we finally drop into bed at night. What do we do Tuesday? We get up and repeat all the rushing of Monday! We eat our lunch in the car on the run. We are going, going, going all day long. The same routine goes on day after day, week after week. In order to have proper homes, however, we must stop the rush long enough to analyze. Our homes will probably not have the improvement they need unless we take time to analyze our problems.

Evaluate what you say. Analyze where you are going. Before Nehemiah ever did anything—before he ever began to nail a nail or put up a stone in the wall—he analyzed. He evaluated. I challenge you to do the same.

Great leaders evaluate. Do you?

CHAPTER 7

CLARITY

*Then said I unto them, Ye see the distress that we are in,
how Jerusalem lieth waste, and the gates thereof are burned
with fire: come, and let us build up the wall of Jerusalem,
that we be no more a reproach.*

                              ❧ Nehemiah 2:17

Introduction

NEHEMIAH 2:17 BEGINS WITH the word *then*. When did Nehemiah speak? After he prayed.
When? After he listened.
When? After he became compassionate.
When? After he was faithful in his present position.
When? After he experienced some loneliness.
When? After he evaluated and weighed the situation.

The next quality of leadership is *clarity.* A leader must be clear. Most leaders are unclear. It is tragic. If we are not careful, we will confuse people; but a good leader will clarify, or make clear, what he is speaking about. He will be concise in all his directions. Parents and businessmen desperately need to be clear when they communicate.

When Nehemiah finally began to address the issue, he was direct, clear, and concise in his communication with his people. He did not beat around the bush.

Many people are simply chatter boxes. They talk endlessly. Instead of chattering on and on, their directions need to be clear, concise, and direct. Nehemiah had been silent for four months.

Now, four months later, he finally began to communicate. Clarity is vitally important.

Nehemiah got right to the point. Let us carefully consider the language of Nehemiah 2:17:

"Then said I unto them, Ye see." His statements were made directly to the people he was addressing. He did not say that he saw they had a problem, he said they had a problem, too. *"Ye see the distress that we are in."* I like the fact that his communications had a team spirit about them. He said, *"the distress that we are in...let us build the wall...that we be no more a reproach."*

Clarity in the Church

Every month I meet with our deacons. The secretary types out my agenda for them. I begin by saying that first of all, we are going to talk about this subject. Secondly, we are going to talk about this subject. Thirdly, we are going to talk about this subject. Finally, we are going to talk about this subject. I always have my agenda printed out for them, so they can see it. When we get to a certain subject, I clearly convey the matter to be considered. For example, if the subject of missionary support arises, I make a statement like this: "There's a man who is going to start a church in Newark. His name is Dwight Tomlinson. I would like to recommend that we support him. Now, let's talk about it." I have found out that it is a lot better to announce what you are thinking about and then explain it. This makes deacons' meetings and church business meetings much better.

Unfortunately, most people do not do that. Most people explain the topic, and then they announce what they want. That method always come back to haunt them because it breeds confusion. While you are explaining the subject, people are trying to interpret what you want. They may be wondering whether you want to take the guy on for support or not. You finally say, "And by the way, I think we ought to take him on for support." When you finally say you think this missionary should be supported, the deacons have already evaluated your words, and have developed the idea that they should not take the missionary on for support because they thought you were saying something different the entire time.

Clarity with Children
The same thing is true with our children. *Say exactly what is on your heart, and then explain it.* We should be clear and concise with our children. Many times our children disobey us, because they simply do not know what we want, because what we want changes so much from day to day.

Here is what most parents do—they jerk their child. They spank him and say they are upset with the child. After all that, then the parents finally try to get to the root of the problem. This is wrong. First, discover what the problem is. When parents have something to say, they should say it fast and in a clear and concise manner so the child knows what the parents are talking about.

Nehemiah did that. He was saying that they were in trouble. The city was in trouble. Let's build. A careful reading of Nehemiah 2:17 demonstrates this. When he said, *"Ye see the distress that we are in,"* he was saying that they were in trouble. When he said, *"Jerusalem lieth waste,"* he was saying that the city was in trouble. Let's go build.

Developing Clarity
Prepare what you are going to say ahead of time. Nehemiah knew what he was going to say because he had waited and prayed for four months.

Be clear and concise in what you say. Nehemiah first identified the problem. He said in Nehemiah 2:17, *"Ye see the distress that we are in, how Jerusalem lieth waste, and the gates thereof are burned with fire."* Then he clearly announced a remedy, a plan for that problem. Be clear. Be concise.

Have the person being instructed repeat back to you what you said. To be sure you have been clear, have the person you have just instructed repeat back to you what you have said. That would be a good thing in the home. For example, a father might ask, "Son, now what did Dad say?"

Do not say too much. In order to have clarity in conversations, do not say too much. We parents oftentimes have too many rules. It is better to limit the number of rules, but make the rules count. Do not just rattle on and on. Be clear. Be concise.

Examine Nehemiah's communication once again. After being quiet for four months, he said,

> *Ye see the distress that we are in, how Jerusalem lieth waste, and the gates thereof are burned with fire: come, and let us build up the wall of Jerusalem, that we be no more a reproach.*
>
>   ❧ Nehemiah 2:17

As far as I am concerned, that is simple, direct, and clear. Be clear and concise!

Great leaders use clarity. Do you?

CHAPTER 8

CONFIDENCE

Then I told them of the hand of my God which was good
upon me; as also the king's words that he had spoken unto
me. And they said, Let us rise up and build. So they
strengthened their hands for this good work.

                              ❧ Nehemiah 2:18

Introduction

CONFIDENCE IS A VITAL QUALITY of leadership. Webster's dictionary says confidence is simply a firm belief; assurance; certainty, being certain. *Vine's Expository Dictionary,* a Greek dictionary, defines the word *confidence* as boldness. A leader must have a firm belief. A leader must be confident.

Today, people want to find confidence in someone who knows where he is going. People are looking for someone to follow. Confidence does not mean arrogance or pride; but it does not mean a false humility either.

It is not wise for a new pastor to announce that he is not worthy to be a pastor. Of course he is not worthy! No one is worthy; but God can equip him for the task. After we elected Mr. Reagan to the office of Commander in Chief of our armed forces, he ordered our men to invade Granada. He also sent our aircraft to bomb Libya. The Senate said he had no right to do that. He should have had a Senate hearing on that. Despite that political opposition, Mr. Reagan exhibited great confidence.

Be confident in your leadership. A leader is one who sets the direction. Some leaders fret about what will happen if people do not like their direction. I can assure you of one thing: they probably will not like your direction, but you should not allow that to rob you of your confidence.

Place No Confidence in Your Flesh

In Philippians 3:3, Paul says about glorying in the flesh, *"We...have no confidence in the flesh."* As the songwriter said, "The arm of flesh will fail you." Do not say, "I can do it. I can do it." That is the world's philosophy today. That is why there are symposiums and conferences at hotels almost every week about the positive approach to thinking. These worldly advisers say to believe in yourself! You can accomplish it! You can do it! You'll make it! This kind of thinking is completely wrong. Paul told us not to place any confidence in the flesh. The flesh will fail you. Do not place your confidence in the flesh.

Place Your Confidence in the Lord

Notice the phrase *"the hand of my God which was good upon me"* (Nehemiah 2:18). Nehemiah was saying that he was nothing. He was just a cupbearer. But even though he had no confidence in his own flesh and his own ability, he had confidence in the Lord because God's hand was upon him. Nehemiah demonstrated true confidence; he had an assurance in God's power.

Psalm 118:8, the middle verse in the Bible, says, *"It is better to trust in the LORD than to put confidence in man."* God wants us to have confidence, but He wants our confidence to be in Him, not in man. The Bible says, *"I can do all things through Christ which strengtheneth me"* (Philippians 4:13).

Romans 8:37 says, *"We are more than conquerors through him that loved us."* By placing our confidence in the Lord we develop boldness. We manifest confidence when we think that we can do it with the help of God. We can do it because we are on God's side. We can do it because *"I can do all things through Christ which strengtheneth me"* (Philippians 4:13). You can be the right father. You can be the right mother. You can be the right employer, the right employee, the right leader. Through Christ we are more than conquerors.

The patriarchs spoke with confidence. The judges spoke with confidence. The kings spoke with confidence. The prophets spoke with confidence. The apostles spoke with confidence. Why? Their trust was in the Lord.

Hebrews 11 is about confidence. Godly people were able to subdue kingdoms through Christ. They were able to break down walls through Christ. They were able to defeat armies through Christ. They were able to slay a bear and kill giants through Christ. *"I can do all things through Christ"* (Philippians 4:13).

Be Slow to Place Confidence in Man

I did not say you should not place confidence in man because that would be contrary to the teaching of the Bible. You must place confidence in leadership, but you should be slow in placing confidence in leadership. You should not jump at the first job offer. You ought to make sure you can work in an area, considering the employer, manager or foreman who will be over you. You should not accept a job quickly just because the pay is good. Good pay is worth nothing if you cannot place confidence in the leadership. Who cares how great the pay is if it gives you ulcers, gets you upset, and unnerves your family? It is vitally important that you have confidence in the people who will employ you.

Great leaders are confident. Are you?

CHAPTER 9

INVOLVEMENT

And they said, Let us rise up and build. So they strengthened their hands for this good work.

ᐨ Nehemiah 2:18

Introduction

NEHEMIAH'S NEXT LEADERSHIP QUALITY was total *involvement.* People were involved in the construction of a place the Bible calls the fish gate; others worked on the water gate. (Watergate was in the Bible long before President Nixon was involved with it!) None of the gates were very glamorous. One group of people had the responsibility of working on the dung gate where all the manure was removed from the city. We see that Nehemiah aimed for total involvement.

It is critically important that leaders learn to involve as many people as possible in the projects they pursue. You should not, for example, just have a home based on the father. Certainly he needs to be the leader of the home, but dad ought not to be the only one in the home to whom everyone bows down. You ought to have the entire family as a unit. Everyone should be involved.

Sometimes a wife is treated as a slave. We treat our wives as slaves when we say, "There are the kids' beds; go make them." This is wrong. Even in the home there needs to be total involvement. The children need to start learning how to make beds. If they start making their beds at the age of four or five, they are not going to do a good job. It would be a rare thing if a child four or five years old could make his bed military style. You would have a very unusual son if he could make his bed like that at age four; nonetheless, he should be involved in those things.

I was in Canada preaching recently, and while I was there I met a little boy who was probably the most intelligent little boy I have ever met in my life. He was five years of age. He spilled some orange juice on the table cloth in the morning at breakfast, turned to his mother, and, at age five, said, "Mother, I have just soiled the table cloth." A five-year-old boy! He "soiled" the table cloth! I learned that he read a page of the dictionary every day. He loves it! His dad told me this story:

A preacher who was a guest in their home said to the young man's father, "Tell us, Brother, when did you get saved?" The father said he had been saved in the early 70's, and talked about his salvation. The boy had never heard about his father's salvation before, and he said, "Excuse me, Father, may I interrupt?" The dad said, "As soon as I'm finished I'll let you talk." He finished, and then said, "All right, son, what do you have to say?" The boy said, "Dad, I was figuring out when you got saved. Were you saved during the Vietnam War?" That boy had a brilliant mind. When the father told me this incident, I scratched my head and wondered if the Vietnam war were in the 80's or 90's! That little boy knew. I do not think that he and I would get along too well!

Even though few children are as intelligent as that five-year-old boy, you should make every effort to involve your children in your home. Do not just involve the mother, involve everybody. Cut the lawn together. When my children were very young, they were not an asset to my work. They really did not help! They slowed me down; but giving them a chance to help with tasks around the house was a great help to them. You should not tell your kids to just leave you alone. Get them involved, for their sake.

Nehemiah wanted his people to be involved. He recognized that if the job were going to get done, it could not be a one-man show. They built a wall around their city, and the Bible declares that Nehemiah so organized the work and so involved the people that they did it in fifty-two days. He told them the direction where they were going, how it was going to be accomplished, and asked if they would help. They said they would.

How Should You Involve Others?

To involve others, be a leader, and reveal to people by your actions that you know where you are going. People want to follow someone that knows where he is going. Employees want to follow a leader that knows where he is going. Whether you like him or not, I understand that Mr. Iacocca has changed the Chrysler Corporation. He turned around a bankrupt company. Mr. Iacocca told the corporation what they were going to do, where they were going to go, and how they were going to get there. He encouraged them to join the team, and he got people to join the team instead of abandoning ship. They saw a man and realized he knew where he was going.

What is so distressing for so much of the American public today is that it seems we have been offered candidates who are not really leaders. This country is in great need of a President who has built something. Most of the men who have run for President in recent years have never built anything. They have never been president of a corporation. They have never run a company. They have never founded a company. Basically, most of them have been professional politicians. Sadly, many people in top positions of government have never done anything that demonstrates they are capable of leading.

To involve others, lay some groundwork. Nehemiah laid some groundwork. He did everything he was supposed to do; thus, by the time he asked the people to work, a plan was already set. He knew what the people were going to say. People will not get involved if you just simply spring something on them.

For example, our church had a unanimous vote for a building project because we did not just spring it on the church. Throughout the year before we built, we were fasting and praying. On September 18, while I was sitting in a certain chair, God gave clear direction as to what we were to build. Four months later, I presented it to the people and asked them to help build it. You must lay some groundwork.

We often fail to lay proper groundwork in our homes. When we want to get our wives and our children involved in some project, we normally just spring it on them. Instead, we should plan ahead and lay some groundwork.

Some people get all pumped up when someone preaches against television. A man may say you're wrong if you have a TV. Even if he has decided to remove the television from his home, it is not generally wise to go home and say, "All right, I'm making a decision. We're getting rid of the TV." Though I do not think television offers much, it may be that his family did not hear the message. Maybe they heard it, and they did not like it. Before he quickly removes the television from his house, he should lay some groundwork. Perhaps he should discuss with his wife some of the things on television that are of bad character, things which do not build the proper qualities in a family. Perhaps he should confess that some of the programs have had an ill effect on him. He should suggest to his wife that they should start praying about this issue every night. If he is sure the television should be removed from the house, laying groundwork will make the process much smoother.

You see, things go in fads in churches. Somebody says, "Well, this family doesn't have a TV, so we're getting rid of our TV." That is the wrong reason to get rid of your television, because you will get it back someday if you base your decision on what some other family has done. When leaders lay groundwork, they are less likely to make decisions for the wrong reasons. I do not think it is fair to our children when we make decisions for them without even thinking about them and bringing their needs into the decision-making process, though certainly there ought to be many decisions we just simply make. Without laying the proper groundwork, we just come home one day, and, because the television was on for twelve hours the day before, we say, "It's over. It's done. I'm putting my fist through it. We're getting rid of it." Oh, how careful we need to be to lay some groundwork.

The same thing would be true in marriage, and that is where many of our children go wrong. Preparation is involved in courting and dating. You should not just say one day that you are in love and get married the next day. There has to be preparation. You have to lay some groundwork.

To involve others, be direct. Nehemiah 2:17 says, *"Then said I unto them."* Tell them. When Nehemiah said, *"Let us build the wall,"* he was saying that he needed their help. People rally to you when they think you need them. I want to use the pulpit to build the lives of my church members; but if our church goes forward, the members need to be involved also. When somebody gets mad and disgruntled, another member sometimes says that the church didn't need him anyway. Nothing could be further from the truth. We need our people, and we need to involve them in our work.

Why Should You Involve Others?

When you involve others, you can accomplish more. When I first came to Santa Clara, I was the church's only staff member. The first staff member I hired was my wife for $25 a week when we could afford to pay her. She worked 40 hours a week for $25. From that point, there came a time when I realized that we needed to hire more people if we were going to go further. We added Brother Carey first, and then we gradually added others. The Bible says in Deuteronomy 32:30, *"How should one chase a thousand, and two put ten thousand to flight."*

When you involve others, it gives people a sense of belonging. People need to belong to something in life. There is happiness for them when they are not doing their own thing.

It is Biblical to involve others. Gideon involved three hundred soldiers. Nehemiah involved many, many people in the building of the wall. David involved his mighty men. Moses involved his seventy men. Jesus involved His twelve disciples. The early church involved its one hundred twenty people.

Why You Do Not Involve Others

Why don't we involve others? Why don't we involve our children in our home? Why don't we involve our wives? Why don't we involve our husbands with our decisions? Why don't we involve our employees? Why don't we involve our church members?

We don't involve others because of fear. We are afraid. We fear that if we involve them, it may be revealed that a follower knows more than the leader. We should realize, however, that your follower does know more than you sometimes.

We don't involve others because of pride. Too often we think we want all the glory. We don't want to share the glory with anybody. I'm the pastor around here! You may be the pastor; but with that approach, you are going to pastor yourself if you are not careful!

Before Jim Carey came on our staff, I received all the attention and all the gifts. Before his coming, I received all the notes—and all the chocolate chip cookies with walnuts. My human nature did not want to share these benefits with someone else, but I realized that it was necessary to overcome pride so the work could be furthered.

I can recall Brother Hyles talking about his first staff member. He said, "One day I was coming out of my driveway, and my car went off into the grass and got stuck in a snowbank. I was spinning my tires back and forth, and I burned up the transmission. A staff member came by and began talking with me."

"Hey, are you stuck?" he said.

Dr. Hyles said, "No, I'm just playing in the snowbank here. I just love to do it. I just love doing these things."

And he said, "Looks like you're stuck, Preacher."

Brother Hyles said, "I'm stuck, and I've also burned up the transmission."

The staff member said, "That's too bad. Do you know what you need, Pastor? You should have those bald tires taken off, and you need some snow tires."

Brother Hyles said, "I know I need snow tires, but I can't afford snow tires. I don't have any money for snow tires."

The staff member said, "Say, that's too bad."

Brother Hyles said he turned and looked at the staff member's car and said, "Hey, where did you get those new snow tires?"

"You didn't hear? Mr. and Mrs. So and So bought those for me."

Brother Hyles said a green, ugly monster began to rise within him because it is sometimes difficult to overcome selfishness and pride.

I have had the same kind of experience. When I worked for Brother Larry Chappell, there were about fifteen adult Sunday school classes. They all had their parties one night. I went by Brother Chappell's office, and he said, "What did you get for your Christmas gift, Brother Trieber?"

I said, "My class bought me a beautiful lamp."

He said, "I thought so."

Every class except his had bought the teacher something for Christmas. He was feeling low, and I will never forget it.

One year, the exact same thing happened to me. Everybody's class had bought them something, but nobody had bought me anything. That year I do not think I got five gifts total from the church. I was hearing comments like, "What do you get the pastor? He's got everything." I didn't have anything. People were saying, "You know, the pastor gets all the gifts"; but staff members were getting more gifts than I. I went home, and God did a great work in my life. I realized that I did not come on board to get gifts. I came on board to bless the lives of others so that they might receive. When I got that thing settled, it changed Christmas for me. When I think about Christmas now, I sincerely feel that I want my church members to purchase gifts for my staff members instead of purchasing gifts for me. I am so happy when our good people purchase gifts for the staff.

We do not like to involve others because of our pride. We get jealous of them. We should not let fear or pride prevent us from involving others in our work.

Great leaders involve others. Do you?

CHAPTER 10

RIDICULE

But when Sanballat the Horonite, and Tobiah the servant, the Ammonite, and Geshem the Arabian, heard it, they laughed us to scorn, and despised us, and said, What is this thing that ye do? will ye rebel against the king? Then answered I them, and said unto them, The God of heaven, he will prosper us; therefore we his servants will arise and build: but ye have no portion, nor right, nor memorial, in Jerusalem.

◆ Nehemiah 2:19-20

Introduction

CHAPTERS 2, 4, AND 6 OF Nehemiah deal with the fact that a leader will suffer scorn and *ridicule*. Folks will laugh at you. They will not agree with you, and they will be blunt about it. Some will start a campaign against you.

When your business is successful, someone will try to scorn, ridicule, and hurt your business instead of being happy with the success you have had. If we are not careful, the same will be true in our homes. When we see a good home while our home is having trouble, we sometimes begin to scorn and ridicule the family that is doing well in order to make us look better. That happens so often. The same is true in our churches. A church that is solid, growing, and filled with love, is often ridiculed by another church. The same is true of a Sunday school teacher, a deacon, or a staff member. We ridicule, we scorn, we scoff, and we try to discourage him.

Nehemiah explained the condition of the city and encouraged them to build together; and the people said, *"Let us rise up and build"* (Nehemiah 2:18). As soon as they said that trouble began. Sanballat, Tobiah, and Geshem laughed at the builders and despised them.

Whenever a church or a person or business says to do something, to rise up and build, the devil and his crowd says to rise up and oppress.

When we say to rise up and build a godly home, the devil says, to rise up and oppress. When we say to rise up and build up a godly business, a good business, a solid business, the devil says to rise up and oppress. In your personal life, perhaps God spoke to your heart. Perhaps you made a decision, walked down the aisle to an old-fashioned altar, got right with God and said, "Oh, God, I want to build on a firm foundation and get my life right with Thee." Before you walked out of the door of the church, the devil was planning to rise up and oppress.

That is the way he works. Moses experienced that; David experienced that; Elijah experienced that; Jesus experienced that; the disciples experienced that; and you and I experience the same. No one likes opposition, but it is part of life. Opposition is going to come. The test of a man's character is not what it takes to get him going, but what it takes to get him to stop. Don't let anything stop you. Get in the direction God would have you to go, and just keep on going.

> I'm pressing on the upward way,
> New heights I'm gaining every day;
> Still praying as I'm onward bound,
> "Lord, plant my feet on higher ground."

Ridicule is not a pleasant part of life, but it is something we must deal with. People sometimes ask me how to handle ridicule. There are six important strategies for handling ridicule.

Point People to Jesus

That is what Nehemiah did. When Nehemiah's enemies laughed and scorned, he answered, *"The God of heaven, he will prosper us"* (Nehemiah 2:20). He was pointing his enemies to God.

A new Christian is sometimes approached by someone who says, "Are you one of those do-gooders? You're one of those Christians? Oh, you mean you're a deacon now? You mean you're a holy roller now?"

If you are not careful, you will throw your coat off and say, "Yeah! Come on, let's fight about it." You should not do that, for it is best not to answer ridicule. You could say, "Yes, I am a Christian. Isn't it wonderful? I hope you're happy for me that I have trusted Christ as my Savior. I found peace finally. I found joy. You know, George, my life had no happiness. I had no contentment. You know that. You saw me before I got saved, and God has brought a joy and a peace to my heart. Aren't you glad I have joy? Aren't you glad I have peace and happiness?"

Nehemiah pointed his enemies to Jesus. He said, *"The God of heaven, he will prosper us"* (Nehemiah 2:20). Point people to Christ with your life, with your testimony, and with your conversation. When you are ridiculed, point people to Jesus.

Don't Quit

Just don't quit. Nehemiah said, *"We his servants will arise and build"* (Nehemiah 2:20). Don't quit. When people ridicule, don't quit.

The enemies of God constantly ridiculed the work Nehemiah was doing. When Sanballat heard about the rebuilding of the wall, he *"took great indignation, and mocked the Jews"* (Nehemiah 4:1). Then, he said,

> *What do these feeble Jews? will they fortify themselves? will they sacrifice? will they make an end in a day? will they revive the stones out of the heaps of the rubbish which are burned?*
>
> Nehemiah 4:2

Tobiah the Ammonite was by him, and he, too, ridiculed the Jews, saying,

Even that which they build, if a fox go up, he shall even break down their stone wall.

                                  ❧ Nehemiah 4:3

The fox is the lightest of walking creatures. A fox can walk and hardly move a leaf. Sanballat was saying that even if a fox walks on that wall, it's going to break down. He began to ridicule and scoff.

This ridicule greatly affected the Jews. In Nehemiah 4:4-5, they prayed, *"Hear, O our God; for we are despised,"* and *"cover not their iniquity."* In spite of their feelings about this ridicule, they could say, *"So built we the wall"* (Nehemiah 4:6). Don't quit.

You say that they are ridiculing us; they are making fun of us; they are scoffing at us. I know, but don't quit. We are living in a day of quitters, but don't quit. Someone else may ridicule your business, but don't quit. Just keep on going. If someone ridicules your family, don't quit.

Nehemiah 5:1 describes a great cry going out while the wall was being built. People began to get discouraged. In spite of this Nehemiah was able to say,

Yea, also I continued in the work of this wall, neither bought we any land.

                              ❧ Nehemiah 5:16

He did not spend his time buying land and building his own house. He spent the time on the project that God told him to build—the wall. He just kept building the wall. His continued work in the face of ridicule enabled them to finish the wall. As Nehemiah 6:15 says so forcefully, *"So the wall was finished."*

Just keep at it. Don't quit. Don't quit when you have been ridiculed.

Don't Quit

When things go wrong, as they sometimes will,
When the road you're trudging seems all uphill,
When the funds are low, and the debts are high,
And you want to smile, but you have to sigh,
When care is pressing you down a bit,
Rest, if you must—but don't you quit.

Success is failure turned inside out—
The silver tinge of the clouds of doubt—
And you never can tell how close you are,
It may be near when it seems afar;
So stick to the fight when you're hardest hit—
It's when things seem worst that you mustn't quit.

I am sure you have sometimes felt like quitting. I have had many conversations with people and their children, and I have heard things said that had no business being said. I have heard children say mean and ornery things, things that hurt. I have heard children scorn, ridicule, and scoff at their parents. I grieve for those parents; but parents, don't quit. Just keep on going.

How careful we need to be in business. People will scoff at you and scorn you; things sometimes will not go right, and it sometimes gets so hard that you want to quit. Don't quit! In the church, in the home, at school, at work, or wherever it may be, just don't quit.

We are living in a day of quitters. Our school soccer team played a game, and the score was 0 - 0 when the clock ran out. After overtime and double overtime, the score was still 0 - 0. The opposing coach said to our coach to just call it a draw, and to quit for today.

Our coach told him that we were not going to call it a draw because we didn't believe in tying. Then our coach quoted the great Vince Lombardi, "Tying is like kissing your mother-in-law." We don't want to tie. Mr. Lombardi also used to say, "I'd rather lose than tie." Finish it. Stay until somebody wins. Our coach said that we were not going to have a tie, we would have a shoot-out. Five of their guys tried and five of our guys tried, but no one scored.

The other coach said, "Let's go home. Let's make it a tie."

"No!" our coach said. "Let's shoot it out again." We had five more guys shoot, and they had five more guys shoot. Our last guy, the littlest guy on the team, shot it through—and we won!

Just stick with something. We need a crowd of people who will say, "I'm going to stick with my mate. I'm going to stick with my church. I'm going to stick with my ministry. I'm going to stick with my job. I'm going to just stick."

Realize Ridicule Never Stops

In the second chapter of Nehemiah, the enemies of God laughed the builders to scorn (Nehemiah 2:19). In the fourth chapter, they scoffed all the more. In the sixth chapter, they tried all the more. They just kept it up. Unfortunately, you are going to have opposition until the day you die. You are going to have ridicule until the day you die. If you want to get away from ridicule and scorn, your only option is dying. In this life, ridicule will never stop.

Pray

When Nehemiah was ridiculed (Nehemiah 4:1-3), he began to pray:

Nevertheless we made our prayer unto our God, and set a watch against them day and night, because of them.

❧ Nehemiah 4:9

Since ridicule is never going to stop, we need to pray. Just keep on praying. When you have opposition, ridicule, and scorn, just keep praying. Pray, pray, pray! When you experience ridicule at home—pray. When you experience ridicule at work—pray. When you experience ridicule at church—pray. When you experience ridicule at school—pray. When you experience ridicule in business—pray. Since ridicule will never stop, you should never stop praying.

Don't Be Afraid

I like Nehemiah. He said,

> *Be not ye afraid of them: remember the Lord, which is great and terrible, and fight for your brethren, your sons, and your daughters, your wives, and your houses.*
>
> ❧ Nehemiah 4:14

He was saying to not be afraid. Remember God. And after you remember God, remember your brethren. After you remember your brethren, remember your wives, remember your little kids, remember your house. Don't be afraid. We have something for which to fight. If you have a business and you believe in it, fight for it. You believe that God gave you the mate you have in your marriage, fight for your marriage. Fight for it. Don't give up. Don't quit.

Nehemiah's enemies began to hire people to ridicule him. They hired people to try to get him to join hands in an agreement that was not right.

> *And, lo, I perceived that God had not sent him; but that he pronounced this prophecy against me: for Tobiah and Sanballat had hired him. Therefore was he hired, that I should be afraid.*
>
> ❧ Nehemiah 6:12-13

He realized their plan was to put him in fear.

> *Therefore, my beloved brethren, be ye stedfast, unmoveable, always abounding in the work of the Lord.*
>
> ❧ I Corinthians 15:58

Be steadfast. Get a position and stand there. The Word of God says *"we are more than conquerors through him that loved us"* (Romans 8:37). We are on the conquering side. We should not be afraid.

Don't be afraid of the enemy. Do not start working against the enemy and making plans against the enemy. Just keep on doing what you are supposed to be doing. Do not waste time trying to figure out how to fight an enemy; do not figure all you will have to do or how you will fight back. Do not involve yourself with fighting the enemy that is against your home, or you will spend all your time fighting the enemy instead of building your home.

Remember the Importance of the Work

Nehemiah said, *"The work is great"* (Nehemiah 4:19). I like that. The work that we are doing is not just a little Mickey Mouse Club. It is a great work. Nehemiah said, *"I am doing a great work, so that I cannot come down"* (Nehemiah 6:3).

Nehemiah's opponents said to come down. They wanted to meet together and have détente. They wanted a Geneva summit. They wanted to get together and talk about their differences.

Never lose sight of the work you are doing. Get up in the morning and look at your personal life. It is a great work to live for God. People may scoff at you, but you are still doing a great work. They may ridicule your family, but you are still doing a great work. Keep at it. Keep building the family. Keep building the work. Keep building the business. Keep building the church. It is a great work from which you *"cannot come down"* (Nehemiah 6:3).

Great leaders are ridiculed. Are you?

CHAPTER 11

DELEGATE

*Then Eliashib the high priest rose up with his brethren the
priests, and they builded the sheep gate; they sanctified it,
and set up the doors of it; even unto the tower of Meah
they sanctified it, unto the tower of Hananeel. And next
unto him builded the men of Jericho. And next to them
builded Zaccur the son of Imri.*

৵ Nehemiah 3:1-2

Introduction

I
N NEHEMIAH 3:1, MENTION is made of the sheep gate. They
sanctified the sheep gate and set up the doors. As the
chapter continues, many other gates are mentioned, such as the
fish gate, the dung gate, and the water gate. All these gates were
built into the wall.

In verse 2 we read, *"And next unto him builded the men of
Jericho."* In verse 4, the phrase *"And next unto them"* appears at
the beginning, in the middle, and at the end of this verse. Verse 7
says, *"And next unto them."* In verse 8, the phrase *"next unto
him"* is used twice. Verses 9 and 10 say, *"And next unto them."*
Especially notice this phrase from verse 10, *"over against his
house."* Verse 12 again says *"And next unto him."*

Verse 1 speaks of the sheep gate; in verse 3 is the fish gate; in
verse 14 is the dung gate; and verse 32 mentions the sheep gate.
Verse 17 says, *"Next unto him."* Verse 19 says, *"And next to
him."* In verse 28, notice the words *"over against his house."*
That is the second time that phrase has been used. Verse 28 speaks

of the horse gate and contains the third usage of the phrase *"over against his house."* In verse 29, *"over against his house"* is used again. In the last part of verse 30, note the phrase, *"over against his chamber."* Verse 32 finally mentions the sheep gate.

I have taken time to go through those gates because all those phrases are significant to this chapter as we consider the importance of the next ingredient of leadership. The phrases you should note are *"next unto him,"* *"over against his house,"* and *"next to them."* The word *next* is important, and the various types of gates are also important.

If we are not careful, we will read Nehemiah 3 as we do a genealogy. This chapter deals with the quality of **delegation.** If we are going to be successful in business, at home, or in church, we are going to have to learn to use this key of success, delegation. It is critical for those around us, and it is critical for you and me. Webster's dictionary definition of delegation is to assign responsibility and authority to others. We do not give out responsibility alone, but it is critical that we give some authority along with the responsibility. The word *delegation* is vital in a church, in a home, and in a school. It is important in every area. Nehemiah knew how he was going to delegate. He did not know this because he had a board meeting; believe me, it had nothing to do with that. He knew because he went out and evaluated during the nighttime. He took no one with him, got by himself, looked at the condition of the city, prayed night and day, and finally formulated in his mind what he was going to do. He got all the people together, challenged them, and said, *"Let us rise up and build"* (Nehemiah 2:18) and *"Ye see the distress that we are in"* (Nehemiah 2:17). After he got their commitment, he told them what needed to be done.

In Chapter 3, Nehemiah began delegating responsibilities. Something Nehemiah said motivated even the high priest and his brethren the priests (Nehemiah 3:1). *"And next unto him builded the men of Jericho"* (Nehemiah 3:2).

Ingredients of Delegation

First, a good leader will never delegate his job. Do not delegate your job away, or there is no sense in keeping you. But you should delegate. To delegate means to assign responsibility and authority. You give authority when you assign the responsibility, so you do not want to assign, delegate, and give away authority for your personal job to someone else, or you are going to be working for the person to whom you delegated the authority. Soon you will be on the outside looking in.

A mother should not delegate the responsibility of being the housewife to her daughter so the daughter has all the authority and responsibility, does all the cooking, and does all the cleaning, or the daughter will have replaced the mother. In such a case, there is no reason for having the mother around anymore, because she has delegated her position away.

Second, a good leader will accept the importance of delegation. A good leader will realize the importance of involving others in his task to get the job done.

Third, a good leader will delegate those things that he cannot do.

Fourth, a good leader will delegate those things that he should not be doing.

When I came to my church in 1976, there were no staff members. I determined there would only be two reasons why I would hire staff: first, I would hire staff if I did not have the time to fulfill a task; second, I would hire staff if I did not possess the necessary expertise in a certain area. That is not a sign of weakness, for we do not know everything. If you have a task that needs to be done, find someone that can do it better than you and employ him. This does not mean that you are not the boss, for you are still the one signing the paycheck. You are still the president of the company, the dad in the home, or whatever your position may be.

For seven years I led the music, and I was the choir director. I led the choir every single Sunday morning, Sunday night, and Wednesday night. It was fun. It was relaxing. I enjoyed making all the different voices blend to make harmony. However, I no longer had the time to devote to the choir and I felt they had developed past my expertise, so I had to find somebody who could fill the position. I hired Brother Condict and really gave a baby of mine away to him. Though I enjoyed leading the choir, it was hard during the services to lead the choir and immediately turn around to tend to other platform responsibilities.

I remember the first bulletins around here because I typed many of them; however, I do not type them any more. We have employed ladies in the office now, and they have computers. Computers are amazing things. I have no idea under God's heaven how to turn a computer on; and please do not say, "Pastor, I'm going to teach you," because I am not interested in learning.

Fifth, a good leader will discover the strengths and pleasures of those to whom he delegates. Find out what your people like to do and where their expertise is, and give them those jobs. That does not mean that they will not have some job they do not like, for this cannot always be avoided. The phrase "next to his house" demonstrates that Nehemiah followed this principle (See Nehemiah 3:10, 23, and 28-30.) Nehemiah thought a worker would probably like to be building a wall next to his house because his heart was there. The worker would not want to go across the city every morning and work somewhere over there; he would want to work next to his house, for his heart was by his house. If you have somebody who is strong in an area, do not put him in an area where he is weak. Learn the interests of your people, and put them in positions where they are strong.

Great leaders delegate. Do you?

CHAPTER 12

PERSEVERANCE

So built we the wall; and all the wall was joined together
unto the half thereof: for the people had a mind to work.
But it came to pass, that when Sanballat, and Tobiah, and
the Arabians, and the Ammonites, and the Ashdodites,
heard that the walls of Jerusalem were made up, and that
the breaches began to be stopped, then they were very
wroth, and conspired all of them together to come and to
fight against Jerusalem, and to hinder it. Nevertheless we
made our prayer unto our God, and set a watch against
them day and night, because of them.

                                    ✌ Nehemiah 4:6-9

Introduction

THE WORD FOR THIS CHAPTER is ***perseverance.*** It means to stick to it, to keep on keeping on. *"So built we the wall,"* Nehemiah said, *"for the people had a mind to work"* (Nehemiah 4:6). Though the enemies of God all conspired together to fight against Jerusalem and to hinder the work, Nehemiah said, *"Nevertheless we made our prayer unto our God, and set a watch against them day and night, because of them"* (Nehemiah 4:9).

When I was in Bible college, my father wrote to me and oftentimes signed his letter "Dad." Then he would add, "P.S. Keep on keeping on." Don't quit. Hang in there. It is like that picture you have probably seen of the cat that is just barely hanging on to a little limb. It says, "Hang in there, baby." That is perseverance. That is tenacity. We need to stick with it. That is what we need today in leadership. Hang on in that business. Hang on in that church.

Make No Provision for Failure

"*So the wall was finished*" (Nehemiah 6:15). The wall got finished by perseverance. Nehemiah made absolutely no provision for failure. He said that he came to do a job. He did not come to ask if folks liked it. He didn't come to see if the government would pat him on the back. He didn't come to see if his people liked it. He came to do a job for God, and He finished the job. "*So the wall was finished*" (Nehemiah 6:15). Nehemiah had perseverance.

There are three ingredients to perseverance: working, praying, and watching. Let us consider each of them.

Working

The people had a mind to work. Their mind was set on work, not play. We are living in a day when our entire society seems to be living for play. So many people want to be party animals, living for the weekends. They ask, "Is it Friday yet?" What's wrong with Monday morning? What's wrong with Tuesday morning? What's wrong with Wednesday morning? Do not spend your life looking for parties and fun. Spend your life looking for work. Get behind a shovel and a pick; till your back yard; plant some corn and beans. Work!

Praying

They had a heart to pray. The second thing we need if we are going to persevere is prayer. Nehemiah 4:9 says, "*Nevertheless we made our prayer.*" They had a mind to work. Their mind was set on work. They had a heart to pray. The first chapter of this book deals with the tremendous importance of prayer. Prayer is vital, and it helps us to realize we must persevere. Prayer helps us say that we are not going to quit. We are going see it through. We need to learn, first of all, to have a mind to work, followed by a heart to pray.

O what peace we often forfeit,
O what needless pain we bear,
All because we do not carry
Everything to God in prayer!

The songwriter asked, "Ere you left your room this morning did you think to pray?" Perseverance means a mind to work and a heart to pray.

Watching

Nehemiah persevered because he had a mind to work, a heart to pray, and *an eye to watch.* The word *watch* means to have an open eye. We find that the builders *"set a watch against them day and night, because of them"* (Nehemiah 4:9). Every mother needs to keep her eye on her children and her home constantly. Every father needs to keep his eye on his family. Nehemiah kept people watching.

That is what Jesus declared when He ascended to heaven. He told us to watch. He told us to keep our eyes open. Watch! Look! Keep a watch! Watch! Be alert! Watch! Matthew 25:13, Matthew 26:41, I Thessalonians 5:6, and I Peter 4:7 tell us to watch. We should keep our eyes wide open. If we are going to persevere, we will just have to keep at it. We should not quit. We must keep our eyes open. Nehemiah was a man who persevered because he had a mind to work, a heart to pray, and an eye to watch.

Great leaders persevere. Do you?

CHAPTER 13

FINISH

So built we the wall; and all the wall was joined together unto the half thereof: for the people had a mind to work.

          ∾ Nehemiah 4:6

So the wall was finished in the twenty and fifth day of the month Elul, in fifty and two days.

          ∾ Nehemiah 6:15

Introduction

THIS CHAPTER DEALS WITH A leadership quality of *finishing*. Finish the task. If you are going to be a good leader as a husband, wife, father, mother, pastor, church member, or business person, you are going to need to finish some things. We are living in an era when many people do not finish. They start and have fun, but they do not finish. Starting the task is not the important thing; the important thing is finishing the task. Finish the task.

The halfway point is probably the most critical time in a building project. Nehemiah 4:6 says, *"So built we the wall...unto the half thereof."* It is the most critical time in a life. It is the most critical time in a child's life. It is the most critical time of work in the week. It is the most critical time in the day. The middle time, the middle of the day, the middle of the week, the middle of life—whatever it may be—is the critical time. In Nehemiah 4, the builders were halfway done, and they still had a mind to work; and in Nehemiah 6 we read, *"So the wall was finished."* Do not make the bed or clean the room halfway. Do not sweep the floor or the sidewalk halfway. Do not clean the car halfway. Do not cut the lawn halfway. Finish the job.

God Finished His Creation

The Scripture says, *"Thus the heavens and the earth were finished"* (Genesis 2:1). That is the first time the word *finish* is used in the Bible. God said He was finished with the heavens, the earth, *"and all the host of them."* He finished all of it. How important it is to finish!

God did not get halfway finished and get tired out. God finished what He started.

Moses Finished His Work

On their way to the Promised Land, the Jews needed a house in which to worship God; so God instructed them to make a tabernacle. The tabernacle was not permanent. It was like a tent structure which could be put up and taken down as they moved from place to place.

> *And he reared up the court round about the tabernacle and the altar, and set up the hanging of the court gate. So Moses finished the work.*
>
>   Exodus 40:33

Moses finished the work; he finished the tabernacle. It is work to finish. Moses said he finished what he started.

> *And it came to pass, when Moses had made an end of writing the words of this law in a book, **until they were finished.***
>
>   Deuteronomy 31:24

Moses finished the Law. The Law, sometimes called the Pentateuch, consists of the first five books of the Bible: Genesis, Exodus, Leviticus, Numbers, and Deuteronomy. That is a lot of writing! Moses probably thought he was writing those five books of the Old Testament for God. God gave them to Moses and Moses finished the task.

God finished creation. Moses finished the tabernacle and the Law.

Solomon Finished the Temple

Solomon began to build the Temple (I Kings 6:1), and he finished it. Notice these verses:

So he built the house, and finished it.

             I Kings 6:9

So Solomon built the house, and finished it.

             I Kings 6:14

And the whole house he overlaid with gold, until he had finished all the house.

             I Kings 6:22

And in the eleventh year...was the house finished.

             I Kings 6:38

In addition to building the Temple, Solomon built a house for himself, *"and he finished all his house"* (I Kings 7:1). He finished God's house, and he finished his own house. After Solomon had finished all this building, the Lord appeared unto him again.

And it came to pass, when Solomon had finished the building of the house of the LORD, and the king's house, and all Solomon's desire which he was pleased to do, That the LORD appeared to Solomon the second time, as he had appeared unto him at Gibeon.

             I Kings 9:1-2

Solomon finished the job. In I Kings 9:25, the Bible reminds of this one more time: *"So he finished the house."*

Paul Finished His Course

In the New Testament book of Acts, Paul said he was,

Serving the Lord with all humility of mind, and with many tears, and temptations, which befell me by the lying in wait of the Jews: And how I kept back nothing that was profitable unto you, but have shewed you, and

*have taught you publickly, and from house to house,
Testifying both to the Jews, and also to the Greeks,
repentance toward God, and faith toward our Lord
Jesus Christ. And now, behold, I go bound in the spirit
unto Jerusalem, not knowing the things that shall befall
me there: Save that the Holy Ghost witnesseth in every
city, saying that bonds and afflictions abide me.*

❧ Acts 20:19-23

Paul knew he was going to Jerusalem. He knew what was ahead of him. He knew they would arrest him and put him in bonds. He knew there would be afflictions. He knew they would beat him. He knew what was ahead of him. *"but none of these things move me, neither count I my life dear unto myself, so that I might finish my course with joy"* (Acts 20:24). He knew they were going to beat him and imprison him. He knew he would be shackled and in bondage. He knew that afflictions were awaiting him, but none of those things moved him because when he went into the ministry, he determined he would finish his course. Paul did finish!

For I am now ready to be offered, and the time of my departure is at hand. I have fought a good fight, I have finished my course, I have kept the faith.

❧ II Timothy 4:6-7

Jesus Finished His Work on Calvary
In John's account of our Lord's crucifixion, we read,

When Jesus therefore had received the vinegar, he said, It is finished.

❧ John 19:30

Before the crucifixion, Jesus said, *"I have finished the work which thou gavest me to do"* (John 17:4). While hanging on the cross, He said, *"It is finished."* The Greek word for finished is *tetelestai*, which means paid for in full. Our sin was completely paid for. Jesus finished His job and said, *"It is finished."* Jesus is the completer, the finisher, of our faith.

*Wherefore seeing we also are compassed about with
so great a cloud of witnesses, let us lay aside every
weight, and the sin which doth so easily beset us, and
let us run with patience the race that is set before us,
Looking unto Jesus the author and **finisher** of our faith.*

         🙢 Hebrews 12:1-2

I have heard people say, "I'm not a finisher, but I'm a good starter." There is no such thing as a good starter who does not finish. If you are not a good finisher, you are not a good starter. The question is not whether you can start a job, it is whether you can finish the job.

Think with me of a runner running the four laps of the 440. The first time around, he is way out in front of everybody. Someone comes by as he is running the first lap and says, "How are you doing it? You're a half a lap ahead of everybody."

He says, "I'm a good starter!" In the second lap the other runners are a quarter of a lap behind him. In the third lap they are right up with him. In the fourth lap he is way at the end, and he quits, saying, "I can't finish it, because they beat me."

This runner is not a good runner because he started well; and the fact that he did not finish the race demonstrates that he is not even a respectable runner. If you are not a good finisher, you are not a good starter.

As people approach middle age, they often begin to analyze whether or not they can finish. This is nonsense! Of course they can finish!

In Ezra's day, they laid the foundation for the Temple; but for fourteen years, they never finished it. Haggai came along and said,

> *Is it time for you, O ye, to dwell in your cieled houses,
> and this house lie waste?*

         🙢 Haggai 1:4

Haggai was saying that their houses had beautiful, vaulted ceilings; but the house of God was half completed and in rubble.

Just as the prophet exhorted the Israelites to finish building the Temple, I like to encourage middle-aged people to love and enjoy the middle years of life. Do not have a mid-life crisis. Finish the job.

If they are not careful, Christians who have been saved for a number of years will lose the thrill and excitement that characterized their first years of being saved. Not knowing whether we are in the middle or near the very end of our lives should encourage all of us to finish.

Learning to Finish

You can become a finisher by counting the cost before you start.

> *For which of you, intending to build a tower, sitteth not down first, and counteth the cost, whether he have sufficient to finish it?*
>
>   ᴄᴗ Luke 14:28

If you are going to build something, first sit down and count the cost. To count the cost, ask questions like these:

- Can we finish it?
- Do we have the manpower?
- Do we have the finances?
- Do we have the people that are willing to get behind it and finance it?
- Is the church behind it?
- Has the church voted in favor of it?

I recommend that newlyweds do their best to wait two to four years before they have children. If it does not work this way, it is not the end of the world; but it is better to wait so the newlyweds can get used to each other, get a bank account, get prepared, grow up, mature, and count the cost.

When my father-in-law had just celebrated thirty-seven years as pastor in the same church, we thought about his building process. He started in the basement on Auburn Street in Rockford, Illinois, and then, years later, built the second floor and the auditorium.

Then he built another floor on top of that; then he built another building—and another building. Then he built the parsonage. Then he moved off that property and built another building. He has just completed another 30,000-square-foot building. He counted the cost.

He was a farmer with four children. He left the farm, went into the ministry, went to Bible college with four kids, and began as a farmer, a preacher, and a student all at the same time. He counted the cost. After thirty-seven years, he was still in the same church.

You can become a finisher by having character. Let your character say, "I'm not going to quit."

You can become a finisher by making no provision for failure. Do not have a Plan B in case Plan A does not work.

You can become a finisher by looking to proper examples of finishers. If you want to finish, look to proper examples. In the Bible, look to Jesus, Paul, the apostles, and the patriarchs. Look to great heroes such as your grandparents, Billy Sunday, D. L. Moody, Charles Spurgeon, R. A. Torrey, and Ira Sankey. Look to men of yesterday and people of today who are finishers. Look to your parents if they are finishers. Look to your relatives if they are finishers. Look to men of God. There are many preachers who are excellent examples of finishers.

Great leaders finish the task. Will you?

CHAPTER 14

WORK

So built we the wall; and all the wall was joined together unto the half thereof: for the people had a mind to work.

ɑ Nehemiah 4:6

Introduction

WEBSTER DEFINES **work** as bodily or mental effort exerted on something. Work is toil. Work is labor. Some people do not have a physically demanding job; they have a mental job where they "push a pencil." That is work. Others come home from work all dirty and worn out. That is also work. A child came to our Sunday school many years ago, and I went to visit him. As I was at his home, he said, "What do you do for a living, Pastor?"

"You just named it. I'm the pastor."

He said, "I know you do that on Sunday, but what do you do for a living?"

And I said, "Well, I'm the pastor."

And he said, "No, I know you do that on Sunday, but what do you do Monday, Tuesday, Wednesday, Thursday, Friday, and Saturday? What do you do?"

I said, "I'm the pastor of the church Monday, Tuesday, Wednesday, Thursday, Friday, and Saturday."

"No, you don't get it. Where do you go to work? You don't work as a pastor. What do you do?"

I was going to tell him all that I did; but I decided not to give him a long dissertation he would not have comprehended, and I simply said, "I'm just a pastor, I guess."

He said, "Man, they pay you for that?"

And I said, "Yeah, they pay me for that all right."

The word *work* is found 420 times in the Bible. The following verses describe God's work in creation:

> *Thus the heavens and the earth were finished, and all the host of them. And on the seventh day God ended his work which he had made; and he rested on the seventh day from all his work which he had made.*
>
> ❧ Genesis 2:1-2

In other words, God the Father, God the Son, and God the Holy Spirit spent six days working—which is effort, which is labor, which is toil—to build and create the world. It was effort. It was toil. After six days, God came to a point where He needed to rest, and He rested from His labor. He rested from his work. That is the first time you find the word *work* in the Bible. Shortly after creation, the Bible describes the fall of man.

> *And unto Adam he said, Because thou hast hearkened unto the voice of thy wife, and hast eaten of the tree, of which I commanded thee, saying, Thou shalt not eat of it: cursed is the ground for thy sake; in sorrow shalt thou eat of it all the days of thy life; Thorns also and thistles shall it bring forth to thee; and thou shalt eat the herb of the field; In the sweat of thy face shalt thou eat bread, till thou return unto the ground; for out of it wast thou taken: for dust thou art, and unto dust shalt thou return.*
>
> ❧ Genesis 3:17-19

God told Adam that the life ahead of him was a life of work. Adam worked before this, of course, because God created man to work. God had already given Adam the job of naming the animals.

God did not create man to sit around and be lazy. Man will discourage himself if he is lazy because man was not created to do that. Man was created to work.

Work while you have opportunity. Ecclesiastes 9:10 says *"there is no work...in the grave."*

God despises laziness. In II Thessalonians 3:10, the Bible teaches that if a man will not work, he should not eat. I wish today that our leaders in Washington D.C., and the American people as a whole would capture that idea. Welfare is not the answer for our country. Proverbs 22:13 and Proverbs 26:13-14 speak about how a slothful man lies on his bed, and, like hinges, rolls back and forth. David committed adultery with Bath-sheba because he stayed home when the other men went out to work and fight the battle. In the mornings he slept in; therefore, he was not tired at night. And when he could not sleep at night, he got up and walked around. When he walked around, he saw what he should not have seen. God despises laziness.

Your work follows you. Revelation 14:13 teaches that your works do follow you. Build something that future generations can enjoy. When you are dead and gone, your grandchildren should be able to say, "Grandpa started this." Your works follow you.

Learning to Work
To learn how to work, place yourself under the authority of another who knows how to work. Brother Ed Young is a fine Christian gentleman who is a member of our church and who has done a great deal of work on our buildings. He works like a house afire. I suppose some people think he works so hard because he is so talented. I believe his excellent work ethic has nothing to do with talent. At one time he watched his dad; and I imagine, as a young boy, he picked up nails, carried the saw, and picked up the wood for his dad. Now, at the end of a day, he can look back and say that he earned an honest day's wages.

It must it be very discouraging to receive a paycheck that you know you did not earn. To learn how to work, put yourself under the authority of someone who knows how.

Another fine member of our church is Brother Bordell who is a hard, hard worker. When he joined our staff, he said, "Pastor, I don't know about pastoring a church. I don't know about being a staff member; but if you'll work with me and tell me what to do, I'll listen."

I have enjoyed working with him because he has just listened. He does not get defensive; he listens. I am not so much smarter than he is, but I have fifteen years of experience in the ministry that he does not have. Someday, he may know more than I; but it is a tribute to his character that he placed himself under the authority of another. Place yourself in a position where you are willing to be taught by someone else.

When I was in Bible college, Dr. Cedarholm, the president of the college, said to me, "Jack, don't go start a church. Don't go pastor a church. First, I want you to work for one or two men for two to five years."

I went to work for my father-in-law, Dr. Melvin Swanson; and then I went to work for Dr. Larry Chappell. I will never forget the first Sunday I worked for Brother Chappell. He stood and commented to the church, "This is the best singing we ever had in our church. Man, it's wonderful. Brother Trieber, you've just done a good job." He was so complimentary, and I was so thrilled and excited about it.

I noticed throughout the service that he was writing notes. I did not know why he was writing notes; but the next day, after all the compliments, he called me into his office and said, "Brother Jack, have a chair. I want to tell you all the things you did wrong yesterday." Some people would think that was unkind, but that is what I wanted. I did not want someone patting me on the back; I wanted someone teaching me what I needed to learn, and he taught me.

To learn how to work, realize that you are violating God's Word when you do not work. When you take unauthorized thirty-minute breaks and ninety-minute lunches, when you just talk and sort of goof off, realize that you are violating God's Word. II

Thessalonians 3:10 says, *"if any would not work, neither should he eat."*

To learn how to work, keep your eyes open, and be alert at all times. God gave us one mouth, two eyes, and two ears. The priority is on the ears, but keep your eyes open. Dr. Jack Hyles pastors the world's largest church. When he comes here, he says, "Let's just walk around. Do you mind?" Normally, we walk through every classroom.

I once asked him, "Why do we go around to these classrooms and look?"

He said, "I'm trying to get ideas by looking at bulletin boards and seeing the way you do it."

If you are going to be an effective leader, be observant. Be alert.

To learn to work, just do it. Roll up your sleeves, work from 8:00 to 5:00, and say, "I'm going to give my boss from 8:00 to 5:00," and then work even longer than that.

To learn to work, ask God for help. If you do not know how to work, say, "God, I don't know how to do this. Help me run this business." Say, "I don't know how to pastor this church. Help me, God."

To learn to work, do not talk about how much you work. Normally, people who talk the most about how hard they work, work the least. Just work. Do not say, "I entertained so many people this week, and I baked fourteen pies." Do not tell everybody what you have done; just do it. It is fun to work. We were created to work. Just work. Just get in there, pitch in, and work. Roll up your sleeves and work. Work is toil. Do not say, "I'm so tired at the end of the day." You are supposed to be tired at the end of the day! That is what work is all about. Learn how to work.

Great leaders work. Do you?

CHAPTER 15

DISCOURAGEMENT

*And there was a great cry of the people and of their
wives against their brethren the Jews.*

                       ✺ Nehemiah 5:1

Introduction

THIS CHAPTER DEALS WITH *discouragement.* Some people
are surprised to learn that discouragement is a
leadership quality, but it certainly is. As a leader, you will get
discouraged. Everybody gets discouraged at some time. I have
never yet met a superman or a superwoman who has gone through
life without discouragement. When you are in a leadership
position, you are going to get discouraged. A mother is a leader,
and she will have times of discouragement. A father will have
times of discouragement. Everybody is human and has the
capability of getting discouraged from time to time.

The key of your leadership is how you handle discouragement
when it comes. What do you do with it? Do you allow the
discouragement to control you or do you control the
discouragement in your home, in your business, and in your
Christian walk? Discouragement and heartache come into your
life to make you a better person. Sorrow comes into your life to
make you a better person. It either makes you a better person, or
it makes you a bitter person.

When the wall was being built, there was a time when the Jews
were against one another. They were having, as it were, internal
problems in the church.

*And there was a great cry of the people and of their
wives against their brethren the Jews...Some also there
were that said, We have mortgaged our lands,
vineyards, and houses, that we might buy corn, because
of the dearth. There were also that said, We have
borrowed money for the king's tribute, and that upon
our lands and vineyards...lo, we bring into bondage
our sons and our daughters.*

  Nehemiah 5:1, 3-5

Indebtedness always brings bondage. That is what we are doing in America today. In our American system, we are spending money that we do not have. We should not have deficit spending. One day our children and our grandchildren will pay for it, and it will bring them under severe bondage. They will start to have civil uprising and civil war in our nation.

Two Types of Discouragement

In this passage in Nehemiah, two basic types of discouragement are mentioned: ***personal discouragement*** and ***personnel discouragement.***

Personal discouragement occurs when you are discouraged with your actions, your attitude, or something you did or did not do. When you are disappointed in this manner, discouragement begins to build and get you down.

Personnel discouragement comes from those around you, from coworkers, your wife, your husband, your children, your business people, church leaders, and church people. If you are not careful, you tear yourself down, or you allow others around you to begin tearing you down, and getting you discouraged.

Sanballat and Tobiah did not discourage Nehemiah, but they got to Judah. Judah is the one who was to be the leader of the twelve tribes. He was to be the "top gun," the number one man.

In Nehemiah 4:10,

Judah said, The strength of the bearers of burdens is decayed, and there is much rubbish; so that we are not able to build the wall.

                          ⮜ Nehemiah 4:10

Judah's discouragement is obvious. Nehemiah was saying, "Let's go do it. Man, we will do it. Let's get with it. Let's do it." The foreman on the job, on the other hand, was saying, "We have problems because the burden bearer's strength is decayed." The word decayed means to stumble or to fall or to stagger. Judah was saying, "You know what? Our people are worn out."

As Americans we tell ourselves too often that we are worn out. There are a hundred sixty-eight hours in a week, and we say that we are tired with forty hours of work? Forty hours is one fourth of a week. That means that we have three fourths of the week left for ourselves. That means that we can sleep or sit in freeway traffic for three fourths of the week. There are lots of things that we have to do after work, but we have three fourths of our time in which to do them. Tell your great grandfather that you're worn out from working forty hours a week in your air-conditioned building, and see what his reaction is. We pamper ourselves in this country. If you shake the average man's hand in America (including the preacher's hand), it is soft.

Responding to Discouragement
If a leader responds like his people respond, he is going to fail. If he allows his people to lead him by saying they are worn out, tired, discouraged, and can't do it, then the job will not get done. If the leader says you know the job cannot be done, then it will not be done. People are looking for someone who says that it can be done! Who says you can't build a church in America? Some people think it's hard because these are the last days. I think that ought to make it all the easier because people ought to be able to see how bad it is. They ought to be able to see that they need something, someone, in their lives. You can succeed. You can succeed in that business. You can succeed as a wife. You can succeed as a husband. You can succeed today.

A leader can learn to properly respond to discouragement by examining Nehemiah's responses. These responses are found in the fifth chapter of Nehemiah.

Nehemiah responded to discouragement by getting upset. Nehemiah was *"very angry when I heard their cry and these words"* (Nehemiah 5:6). That is what made him the leader.

People who work for a passive employer know what I am talking about. It frustrates you to death when you work for someone and do not know what he wants. Nehemiah was the leader, and he let his people know right from the start what he thought about the whole mess. The people were saying they were in trouble. They mortgaged their farms, they couldn't eat, they were tired, upset with one another, and going to quit the project. Nehemiah said that he was going to unravel that.

I wish we had some government leader, either a Republican or a Democrat, who would stand up and speak what he believes and believe what he says. Instead, many politicians say one thing when they are with one crowd, and they say another thing when they are with a different crowd. They even seem to have something else to say when they are trying to make the religious crowd feel good. I wish leaders would just say what they believe. If you are against homosexuality, stand up and say homosexuality is sin. The Bible says Nehemiah was angry, and he expressed himself. Leaders let their peers know what they think of discouragement.

Nehemiah responded to discouragement by evaluating again. He analyzed the discouragement. Nehemiah 5:7 says, *"Then I consulted with myself."* He sat down and figured out what he was going to do. He analyzed what he was going to do. If you get discouraged, do not allow your discouragement to control you. Sit down and analyze why you are discouraged. Evaluate it. That takes discipline and character.

Nehemiah responded to discouragement by developing an **immediate** solution. When you are discouraged, develop an immediate solution. At least let people know where you stand. Go somewhere alone and figure out what you are going to do.

Nehemiah knew they were going to solve their problem.

Nehemiah responded to discouragement by keeping his eyes on the goal. At one point, our church was in the midst of a building project in which one particular inspector seemed to take pleasure in failing us with glee. We never passed anything the first time. We could have become discouraged and thought we would never finish. Instead, we looked at the end of the project and realized it would be done.

Nehemiah responded to discouragement by guarding his thoughts. Nehemiah never said that he had had it! He never quit! Nehemiah just kept on keeping on!

> *Whatsoever things are true, whatsoever things are honest, whatsoever things are just, whatsoever things are pure, whatsoever things are lovely, whatsoever things are of good report; if there be any virtue, and if there be any praise, think on these things.*
>
> ～ Philippians 4:8

When you allow yourself to be discouraged, you are thinking on the wrong things.

Great leaders deal with discouragement. Do you?

CHAPTER 16

INTEGRITY

Then I consulted with myself, and I rebuked the nobles, and the rulers, and said unto them, Ye exact usury, every one of his brother. And I set a great assembly against them.

                                   ∾ Nehemiah 5:7

Introduction

IN THIS PASSAGE, WE FIND another quality that a leader must possess is *integrity*. Why did Nehemiah rebuke the nobles? Why did he rebuke the leaders and the rulers? He rebuked them because they were charging usury, which is exorbitant interest. To use some common, everyday language, they were ripping off the people. When Nehemiah learned they were doing this, he consulted with the nobles and the rulers and said,

> *Ye exact usury, every one of his brother. And I set a great assembly against them. And I said unto them, We after our ability have redeemed our brethren the Jews, which were sold unto the heathen; and will ye even sell your brethren?*

                                 ∾ Nehemiah 5:7-8

Nehemiah said they had worked hard to buy their brothers out of bondage. They had worked hard to come back to Jerusalem to build up the wall and the Temple so they could worship their God. They worked hard to pay the taxes to get them out of bondage. They redeemed them. They bought them back. But when they got into their own free country, the leaders put bondage back on. The leaders taxed them again.

> *Also I said, It is not good that ye do: ought ye not to walk in the fear of our God because of the reproach of the heathen our enemies? I likewise, and my brethren, and my servants, might exact of them money and corn: I pray you, let us leave off this usury. Restore, I pray you, to them, even this day, their lands, their vineyards, their oliveyards, and their houses, also the hundredth part of the money, and of the corn, the wine, and the oil, that ye exact of them.*
>
> ᴄᴏ Nehemiah 5:9-11

Nehemiah said what they were doing was not good. Quit this heavy taxation! Stop all that business! Give it back to them!

> *But the former governors that had been before me were chargeable unto the people, and had taken of them bread and wine, beside forty shekels of silver; yea, even their servants bare rule over the people: but so did not I, because of the fear of God.*
>
> ᴄᴏ Nehemiah 5:15

The past governors had *"taken bread and wine"* and let their servants rule the people. Nehemiah said that he was the governor now. The former governor took from them corn and wine and shekels of silver, and he taxed the people and made it hard on them, which is exactly what the former governor did. He used the taxes for himself. Nehemiah went on to say, *"so did not I"* (Nehemiah 5:15). In Nehemiah's honest actions we see the idea of integrity. Nehemiah said the other guys ripped them off. He would not! He said, *"But so did not I because of the fear of God. Yea, also I continued in the work of this wall"* (Nehemiah 5:15-16).

That is wonderful. Nehemiah in a leadership position as governor, quit the heavy taxation, rolled up his sleeves, and kept working with the people. According to Webster's dictionary integrity means honesty or uprightness. A leader must be honest.

Nehemiah thought they needed to be people of integrity, people who told the truth.

Integrity Defined

Integrity means you will not allow another's actions to control your actions. Nehemiah could have just kept ripping those folks off because every other governor did it in the past, and every other president did it. That's just the way it was, and everyone knew it.

Let me bring it down to where the "rubber meets the road." If a man takes some supplies such as pencils from work thinking it is no big thing, he may end up with a whole drawer of pencils that have the name of his company on them and a son who says, "Dad, look at all these pencils we've got from your company. Do they let you do that?"

Should the father say, "Well, son, everyone is doing that at work"? No, petty thievery is wrong even if everyone does it. Integrity means you will not allow another person's actions to control your actions.

Integrity means you will do what's right though it costs. In 1968 and 1969, I worked at Fry's Food Store in Fremont. One of the men I worked for said, "Jack, you are always here on time. But if you are ever running late, just call in; and I'll punch you in. Then just come in. It will be fine, and you will never get docked."

I was a young teenager and that man was older than I, but I can recall saying, "I can't do that."

He said, "Sure, it's okay. That's what we do around here; and if I'm late, I want you to punch me in."

I said, "I couldn't do that."

He said, "We'll just punch you in, and then you come."

I said, "No, I'm not going to do that." After that they began to make fun of me and call me Goody Two-shoes.

When I ran into that man twenty years later, I was sure glad I had been honest with that company, whether he remembered it or not. Integrity costs.

Integrity means you are more concerned that you possess integrity than that others possess integrity. This is an extremely important point. We always want to get the other guy straightened out; but our job is to make sure we have integrity.

Integrity means honesty. Tell the truth. God says people will be liars in the last days (I Timothy 4:2); yet, Christians are commanded to be honest. Honesty is a vital part of integrity.

Great leaders possess integrity. Do you?

CHAPTER 17

REBUKE

Then I consulted with myself, and I rebuked the nobles, and the rulers, and said unto them, Ye exact usury, every one of his brother. And I set a great assembly against them.

&⸽ Nehemiah 5:7

Introduction

IN ORDER TO BE AN EFFECTIVE leader, you need to know what the Bible says about the word *rebuke.* Nehemiah rebuked the nobles. The word *rebuke* means that you take the error you have discovered and bring it to the attention of the person who has erred. That is what people in the computer field do. They try to pinpoint where a problem is and do something about it. When they discover error, they do not walk away from it and not be involved.

As an aged man getting ready to die, Paul said to a young man in the ministry named Timothy, *"Preach the word; be instant in season, out of season; reprove, rebuke, exhort with all longsuffering and doctrine"* (II Timothy 4:2). There are three things that Paul told Timothy to do as he preached: reprove, rebuke, and exhort.

To exhort means "to encourage someone," but notice the words *reprove* and *rebuke.* The word *reprove* means to discover error; thus, this is a preacher's job as he preaches and deals with his people. The Bible points out that pastors are to guard the sheep because wolves come in. The pastor should continually look to make sure error is not coming into the church. The Bible says pastors should reprove and rebuke. A smart businessman is constantly discovering where the breakdown is in the business and then showing his employees where they are going wrong, and how to fix it. Nehemiah discovered that those rulers were stealing from the people; thus, he decided to deal with these difficulties.

Improper Rebuke

Rebuke is dealing with the problem, but there are many methods you should not use. The silent treatment is a wrong method of dealing with a problem. Some people use this method. You can tell they are upset, but you have to read their minds because they will not talk about the problem. You may know that your wife is upset, but you do not know why because she is giving you the silent treatment. Perhaps it is the other way around. You may know your husband is upset because he is sitting in his chair refusing to talk. Do not use the silent treatment to deal with a problem.

Yelling and screaming are wrong methods of dealing with a problem. This is the opposite of the silent treatment. Some of you work for a boss who yells and screams. Instead of talking with you like an intelligent adult, he comes in with a string of words and says, "You stupid idiot. I told you..." Some husbands deal with their wives that way. They would not deal with their secretaries that way, but they deal with their wives that way. Husbands who use this method are fools!

Ignoring the problem and thinking it will go away are wrong methods of dealing with a problem. Problems do not go away. If your employees are not following orders, if they are standing around talking and sipping coffee all day, that problem is not going to go away unless someone rebukes, unless someone deals with the problem.

Becoming bitter is a wrong method of dealing with a problem.

Proper Rebuke

Rebuke is dealing with the problem. After you have discovered the error, you address it.

Before you begin to rebuke, make sure you are the right example yourself. We have a tendency to correct everyone else because of their problems, but in reality a lot of their problems are things that are surfacing in our own lives.

Know what and how you are going to rebuke before you do it. Most of us are reaction oriented. We see people do something wrong, and we react without thinking it through. Nehemiah was mad when he heard what was going on. He said, *"I was very angry"* (Nehemiah 5:6). Apparently, his veins were popping out; but before he began to open his mouth, he consulted with himself. He thought the thing through.

Get to the point. When you rebuke someone, get to the point. I would not like to work for a boss who did not get directly to the point. I would rather have a boss say, "Jack, you're here in my office today because we have a little problem with your work; and I want to talk to you about it." I would rather have him be candid with me, tell me the difficulty, and get it resolved.

Rebuke in love. As we discover error with our children, let us rebuke in love. We should not "jump down" on them and say, "What's wrong with you kids? You're just a bunch of rebellious, rotten kids." When you say that, you just lost them. You did not get anywhere with them.

Resolve the problem. Get it resolved. Do not leave angry. Do not walk out and slam the door. Get the problem resolved.

Accepting Rebuke

When you are rebuked, receive it as instruction. Learn from it. Your boss may want to talk to you about your work. It's not up to performance standards. You should not become defiant or blow up. Sit down and listen. The reason he is your boss is so he can supervise and correct your actions. Listen. Receive his rebuke as instruction.

When you are rebuked, receive it as discipline. Take rebuke as discipline. By the way, that is what keeps your heart tender. Be able to admit you were wrong.

When you are rebuked, receive it with humility. By nature, we are proud creatures. In the Bible, pride is one of the seven things God hates. In fact, in Proverbs 6 the Bible lists pride as the first of the seven things that God hates.

When you are rebuked, receive it with loyalty. Don't start a campaign against the boss at work. Don't start a petition. Don't start a hate campaign.

Great leaders rebuke their followers. Do you?

CHAPTER 18

CONVICTION

*Now it came to pass, when Sanballat, and Tobiah, and
Geshem the Arabian, and the rest of our enemies, heard
that I had builded the wall, and that there was no breach
left therein; (though at that time I had not set up the
doors upon the gates;) That Sanballat and Geshem sent
unto me, saying, Come, let us meet together in some
one of the villages in the plain of Ono. But they thought
to do me mischief. And I sent messengers unto them,
saying, I am doing a great work, so that I cannot come
down: why should the work cease, whilst I leave it,
and come down to you?*

                                           ꙮ Nehemiah 6:1-3

Introduction

THIS CHAPTER DEALS WITH *conviction.* Conviction comes from
a root word that means convinced. Nehemiah was a man
of conviction. Nehemiah was involved in doing a good work for
God, and could not stop. Conviction is unwavering belief. A
conviction is something you would die for.

By the way, everyone ought to have some things he would die
for. There are certain things I would die for. There are certain
people I trust, by the grace of God, I would die for. The Lord
Jesus died for all kinds. He died for sinners. I would not die for
just anybody, but there are some folks for whom I would die. A

conviction is something you would die for. It is an unwavering belief, something you believe with certainty.

There are many things I would not die for. I would not die for my automobile. It is not a conviction that I drive an automobile. It is a convenience. It is a pleasure. It helps me in work, but I do not have a conviction that I must drive an automobile. I would not die for my house. I could rear my family in a tent if I had to.

In every church, there is a certain element that is out to destroy the church. In every organization, we have to be careful that we do not get involved with the people who are out to destroy. The Bible says that Sanballat, Tobiah, and Geshem got together and said to Nehemiah that he should come on down and meet in the village. They wanted to have an ecumenical meeting together. They wanted to talk about the oneness that they had and how they were going in the same direction. That may sound good, but they were going in different directions. These enemies had not changed their tactics. In the fourth chapter of Nehemiah, they had wanted to meet together to talk about it.

Leaders Must Possess Conviction

Every leader must possess a conviction that what he is doing with his life is right. Conviction will keep you happy. Nehemiah saw that his city was in ruins and he determined in his heart to do something about it. He heard the walls were broken down and his city was destroyed, so he determined he was going to be the man to do something about it.

Nehemiah was not a builder. He had no building experience. Nehemiah was not a banker. He had no banking experience. Nehemiah was not a born leader. He was a cupbearer to the king. Though he was neither a builder nor a banker, he had heard that there was a job to do; and he developed a conviction that if there were a job to do, he was going to do it. He was going to get the job done.

Nehemiah possessed conviction. He said, "I am willing to die for what I believe. I am willing to keep going." As a result of that he was attacked. Real convictions will attract, and real convictions will disturb. Every one of the apostles died a martyr's death. They were not listed in *Who's Who*.

The enemies of God just kept pestering Nehemiah to meet with them (Nehemiah 6:1, 6:4-5). When they could not get Nehemiah to meet with them in the village, they hired a man to try to make Nehemiah afraid.

> *Then I sent unto him, saying, There are no such things done as thou sayest, but thou feignest them out of thine own heart. For they all made us afraid, saying, Their hands shall be weakened from the work, that it be not done. Now therefore, O God, strengthen my hands.*
> ✎ Nehemiah 6:8-9

> *Therefore was he hired, that I should be afraid.*
> ✎ Nehemiah 6:13

> *Tobiah sent letters to put me in fear.*
> ✎ Nehemiah 6:19

About 500 years ago, a Roman Catholic priest named John Huss began to search the Word of God and to realize that the confessional booth was not the way to heaven. He realized that candles were not the way to heaven. He realized that he could not forgive sins as a priest. As a Catholic priest, John Huss began preaching the Word of God. The hierarchy told him he must stop preaching. He took them to the book of Romans and showed them how we are saved by the grace of God and by the blood of Christ, not by candles, statues, and confession. He said he could not but preach the Word of God.

He began to write literature, and they called him again and told him he must stop. His church began to grow, people were getting saved, and people were coming. The whole city was turned to Christ, and the hierarchy said to stop!

John Huss could not stop. After they arrested him, they said he could go back. He could have his pulpit. He could do what he wanted. He just could not preach that Jesus is the answer to salvation.

But John Huss could not help but preach that which he had found from the Word of God. And they took him out to the stake, handcuffed him, and gave him one more chance to recant. If he didn't they would burn him alive at the stake.

He said, "What I have taught with my lips, I seal with my blood." John Huss died a man of conviction.

Most People Do Not Possess Conviction

Most people today do not possess a conviction about anything. They are not convinced about anything. Sometimes families that have attended church and served God faithfully just sort of quit on God if their children turn out bad. They were trying to use the church to rear their children for them; and when their children turned out bad, they quit on God. You ought to have the conviction that you will be at God's house whether your children turn out right or wrong. When our children turn out wrong, we start blaming the pastor, the youth pastor, someone else, or even ourselves. We should not blame anyone. If a problem has happened, stay faithful to God.

Some people have encountered financial problems. They were convinced that they ought to attend church until they had financial problems, and then they quit church to go to work on Sundays. We ought to be convinced we are going to the house of God whether we have financial problems or not.

The Results of Nehemiah's Conviction

Conviction caused Nehemiah to begin this unbelievable project. God dealt with his heart, and Nehemiah knew he must do that.

Before you ever attempt to do anything, make sure that it is a conviction that God has placed in your heart. Before you ever attempt to get married, you must know it is the will of God for your life. You must have a conviction that for better, for worse, for richer, for poorer, in sickness, and in health, till death do you part. You should not, even in your heart, think that if it doesn't work out you can separate. Before you ever ask a girl to marry you, or before you ever say yes to a man, have a conviction. Be convinced that this person is the will of God for you. Before you go into full-time service, sit down and count the cost. Make sure you are willing to pay the price.

Conviction caused Nehemiah to stay in the work. Conviction caused him to start, and conviction caused him to stay.

Conviction caused Nehemiah to finish the work. Nehemiah 6:15 says, *"So the wall was finished."* If you have a conviction to start, you should have a conviction to finish. If you do not finish, you never had a conviction to start.

Great leaders possess conviction. Do you?

CHAPTER 19

REWARD

*Now it came to pass, when the wall was built, and I
had set up the doors, and the porters and the singers
and the Levites were appointed, That I gave my brother
Hanani, and Hananiah the ruler of the palace, charge
over Jerusalem: for he was a faithful man, and feared
God above many.*

√ Nehemiah 7:1-2

Introduction

NEHEMIAH DEMONSTRATED THE IMPORTANT leadership quality
of *rewarding* his workers. One of Nehemiah's
brothers named Hanani came to him and told him that Jerusalem
was in ruins. In Nehemiah 7:1, we see Hanani a second time.
Nehemiah gave Hanani and Hananiah charge, or authority, over
Jerusalem because they were faithful men and *"feared God above
many."* When did he give Hanani charge over Jerusalem? When
the wall was built. When the job was done, Nehemiah rewarded
Hanani with a position of leadership over Jerusalem. Because
they labored with him until the wall was finished, Nehemiah
elevated them to positions of authority.

What to Reward

Nehemiah rewarded faithfulness. Faithfulness should be
rewarded. Faithful church members should be rewarded. A faithful
wife needs to be rewarded. A woman needs to reward her faithful
husband. A child who has been faithful needs to be rewarded. A

faithful employee needs to be rewarded. Nehemiah rewarded Hanani "because he was a *faithful man.*"

Nehemiah rewarded godliness. Nehemiah 7:2 says they *"feared God above many."* We have had the privilege of periodically rewarding Mrs. Morris, a lady who served as our church organist. We sent her to Australia and Mexico because of her faithfulness and godliness. I believe our church had a responsibility to enable her to see her children who are serving the Lord as missionaries and whom she saw only once every four years. We rewarded her faithfulness and godliness.

It is so important for us to realize that godliness should be rewarded. In this country, we reward the silliest things. We reward looks. A beauty pageant is nothing but running women across a platform like cattle. It is crazy. There is no reason to reward beauty. Faithfulness and godliness should be rewarded.

Nehemiah rewarded honesty. Hananiah had the courage to give an honest report regarding the condition of their city. He said what it was really like. Nehemiah rewarded his honesty.

Reward the Ordinary
If you are in a leadership position, you ought to reward two things, the ordinary and the extraordinary. The ordinary is that which a child or employee does day after day. It is the normal thing. It is a responsibility. If a child makes his bed day after day, that is his duty. That is the normal. Periodically, the normal should be rewarded. An employee needs to be rewarded for faithful service. Some say one should not be rewarded because one gets a paycheck; however, there needs to be some other things that encourage him to keep on doing the normal.

Reward the Extraordinary
When a boss requires an extra thirty hours of work, meaning they will work seventy hours this week on a project, he should reward his employees by then later giving them a three- or four-day weekend.

How to Reward

Reward with position. Promote someone to a higher position. That is what took place in Nehemiah 7:2. Nehemiah promoted Hanani and Hananiah from the head of the palace to the head of the city. When it is in your power and authority to promote someone who has been found faithful and honest and godly, do so.

Reward with authority. Give authority to people. They are the men in charge. Hananiah was given authority.

Reward with finances. Give your follower a raise, a bonus, or a gift certificate.

Reward with praise. Many times praise is better than money. Tell your employees they are doing a good job. You are proud of them. Praise will go a long way with a child, an employee, or a mate.

Reward with rest periods. Give times of rest. An employer might give a two-hour lunch, half the afternoon off, or Friday off, or three days off.

Reward with additional incentives. Perhaps you could offer a new watch for whoever meets the quota.

Reward with gifts. Rewards are important. A leader learns to reward.

Great leaders reward. Do you?

CHAPTER 20

BIBLE

*And all the people gathered themselves together as one man into the street that was before the water gate; and they spake unto Ezra the scribe to bring the book of the law of Moses, which the L*ORD *had commanded to Israel. And Ezra the priest brought the law before the congregation both of men and women, and all that could hear with understanding, upon the first day of the seventh month. And he read therein before the street that was before the water gate from the morning until midday, before the men and the women, and those that could understand; and the ears of all the people were attentive unto the book of the law.*

                                 ❧ Nehemiah 8:1-3

Introduction

IN THE FIRST SIX CHAPTERS OF Nehemiah, there was one theme: the reconstruction of the wall. In the last seven chapters of the book, we see the re-instruction of the people. It is important to build the lives of people, and Nehemiah started this process with the Bible. The Law was read in the gate *"from the morning until mid-day...and the ears of all the people were attentive unto the book of the law"* (Nehemiah 8:3). The eighth chapter of Nehemiah emphasizes the Law over and over again. Ezra the scribe stood on the pulpit of wood which was made for the purpose, and *"opened the book in the sight of all the people"* (Nehemiah 8: 5). He *"caused the people to understand the law"* (Nehemiah

8:7), and he *"read in the book in the law of God distinctly, and gave the sense, and caused them to understand the reading"* (Nehemiah 8:8). Ezra told the Israelites, *"This day is holy unto the Lord your God; mourn not, nor weep. For all the people wept, when they heard the words of the law" (Nehemiah 8:9).*

The Bible

Nehemiah recognized the immediate need to get the Word of God to the people. The need of our country is getting the Word of God to our people.

> The B-I-B-L-E,
> Yes, that's the Book for me;
> I stand alone on the Word of God:
> The B-I-B-L-E.

George Washington said, "It is impossible to rightly govern a nation and a world without the Bible."

John Quincy Adams said, "So great is my veneration of the Bible that the earlier my children begin to read it, the more confident will be my hope that they will be useful citizens of the country and respectable members of society."

Andrew Jackson said, "It is this book, the Bible, the rock on which the republic stands."

Abraham Lincoln said, "The Bible is the greatest gift that God has given to man."

Woodrow Wilson said, "I ask every man and woman in this audience today that from this day forward they will realize that part of the destiny of America lies in the daily perusal of this great Book."

What Woodrow Wilson said years ago is so important today. He said that the destiny of America lies in the way our people pursue the Bible. The hope of this country does not lie in Washington; the hope of our country lies in God's people getting the Bible back in their hearts, back in their homes, and back in our schools. Madalyn Murray O'Hare renounced the Bible, and our country has lived without the Bible or prayer in our public schools for decades. We are living in a day of debauchery because our nation has turned her back on the blessed Book.

Douglas MacArthur said, "Believe me, never a night goes by but, ever so tired I may be, that I read the Word of God before I go to bed."

Herbert Hoover said, "The whole of the inspiration of our civilization springs from the teaching of Christ and the prophets. To read the Bible is necessary for the American way of life."

Dwight Eisenhower said, "To read the Bible is to take a trip to a far land where spiritually you are strengthened and your faith is renewed."

Read the Bible

Mom, are you reading the Word of God? Dad, are you reading the Word of God? Are you trying to get your children to read the Word of God? School teacher, are you reading the Word of God? Deacon, are you reading the Word of God? My father-in-law often said, "This Book will keep you from sin, or sin will keep you from this Book."

The Word of God will bring you blessings. Psalm 119:2 says, *"Blessed are they that keep his testimonies."* When a leader reads the Word of God, a blessing is in store. The word *blessed* means happy. Do you nag your children and yell at them? Do you nag your husband? Do you get mad at your wife, yell at her, and pick on her? Are you a grumpy employer? If you are not happy, check your reading of the Word of God. Leaders should check their lives to be sure they are in the Word of God.

The Word of God will bring cleansing. Psalm 119:9 says, *"Wherewithal shall a young man cleanse his way? By taking heed thereto according to thy word."* The Word of God cleanses. Certainly every leader needs cleansing. A husband needs cleansing; a wife needs cleansing; employers and employees need cleansing.

The Word of God will bring counsel. As the Psalmist said, *"Thy testimonies also are my delight and my counsellors"* (Psalm

119:24). Psalm 119:105 says, *"Thy word is a lamp unto my feet, and a light unto my path."* The Bible gives counsel and direction.

The Word of God will bring hope. Psalm 119:43 says, *"And take not the word of truth utterly out of my mouth; for I have hoped in thy judgments."* Note Psalm 119:74, *"They that fear thee will be glad when they see me; because I have hoped in thy word."* Psalm 119:18 says, *"My soul fainteth for thy salvation: but I hope in thy word."*

A leader needs hope. Competitors may give you gloom and doom. Other parents may give you gloom and doom; but you need hope, and your hope needs to be anchored in the Word of God.

The Word of God will bring understanding. Psalm 119:71 is a tremendous verse which says, *"It is good for me that I have been afflicted; that I might learn thy statutes."* Many people are afflicted with ailments, aches, and pains; but they do not tell anybody about their suffering. It is encouraging to know that God allows affliction so we can get strength and understanding from the Word of God, for *"The entrance of thy words giveth light"* (Psalm 119:130).

The Word of God will bring an opportunity to meditate.

O how love I thy law! it is my meditation all the day.
                               ❧ Psalm 119:97

Mine eyes prevent the night watches, that I might meditate in thy word.
                               ❧ Psalm 119:148

But his delight is in the law of the Lord; and in his law doth he meditate day and night.
                               ❧ Psalm 1:2

This book of the law shall not depart out of thy mouth; but thou shalt meditate therein day and night, that thou mayest observe to do according to all that is written therein: for then thou shalt make thy way prosperous, and then thou shalt have good success.
                               ❧ Joshua 1:8

The Word of God will bring peace. Psalm 119:165 says, *"Great peace have they that love thy law."* As a leader, you need peace. We are living in a troubled world, and we need peace. Peace cannot be received from a counselor, from a psychiatrist, or from a book; but you can get peace from *The Book*. The newspaper does not provide peace, but you can receive peace as you read the Word of God.

I think it is amazing that, after reconstructing the wall, Ezra and Nehemiah began to instruct the people with the Bible. They constructed a pulpit, and Ezra began reading the Bible. The people responded by saying, *"Amen, Amen"* (Nehemiah 8:6); and revival started to break loose.

Great leaders love the Bible. Do you?

CHAPTER 21

HUMILITY

Now in the twenty and fourth day of this month the children of Israel were assembled with fasting, and with sackclothes, and earth upon them. And the seed of Israel separated themselves from all strangers, and stood and confessed their sins, and the iniquities of their fathers. And they stood up in their place, and read in the book of the law of the Lord their God one fourth part of the day; and another fourth part they confessed, and worshipped the Lord their God.

ᐛ Nehemiah 9:1-3

Introduction

THE OBVIOUS TEACHING OF THESE verses is that a leader needs to possess the quality of *humility.* The children of Israel spent three hours in the Word of God and three hours in prayer. God was dealing with their hearts.

The person who thinks he is humble is the one who is proud. When we think we are humble, we are not. By nature, we are proud, egotistical, arrogant, self-willed, and determined to get our own way. That is the old Adamic flesh. By definition, humility is lying low. The Bible says that Nehemiah got his people together and began to deal with their hearts.

The Bible says the Israelites *"were assembled with fasting"* (Nehemiah 9:1). Fasting requires humility. When you fast, you are denying yourself. You are lying low and instead of caring about eating food, you are caring about praying. Their sackcloth was an example that they were not proud of themselves. They were dressed on the outside in a way that revealed the inside. They stood and separated themselves, and God's people need to be separated. They separated themselves from strangers and people who did not love the Word of God. It would be wise if God's people learned to separate themselves from those who do not love the Word of God. After they separated themselves, they stood and confessed their sins.

The actions of the Israelites described in Nehemiah 9 reveal their humility. In Proverbs 15:33, we read, *"The fear of the LORD is the instruction of wisdom; and before honor is humility."* God will honor you, but before honor is humility. Humility is *lying low,* not broadcasting how great and marvelous you are in all the great things you can do. Proverbs 18:12 says, *"Before destruction the heart of man is haughty, and before honour is humility."* James 4:6 says, *"But he giveth more grace. Wherefore he saith, God resisteth the proud."* God works against the proud, *"but giveth grace unto the humble."* Notice James 4:10, *"Humble yourselves in the sight of the Lord, and he shall lift you up."* I Peter 5:5 says, *"Likewise, ye younger, submit yourselves unto the elder. Yea, all of you be subject one to another, and be clothed with humility."* That verse teaches we are to be dressed with humility. Philippians 2:5-7 says, *"Let this mind be in you, which was also in Christ Jesus: Who, being in the form of God, thought it not robbery to be equal with God: But made himself of no reputation, and took upon him the form of a servant."* Christ humbled Himself.

Steps to Humility
1. Don't talk about yourself.
2. Don't think about yourself. We think of ourselves too much.
3. Never expect anything from anybody.
4. Practice self-denial. Say no to yourself.
5. Follow the lives of humble people.
6. See Jesus. As the writer of Hebrews said, *"Looking unto Jesus"* (Hebrews 12:2).

Great leaders are humble. Are you?

CHAPTER 22

CHURCH ATTENDANCE

*Then contended I with the rulers, and said, Why is the
house of God forsaken? And I gathered them together,
and set them in their place. Then brought all Judah
the tithe of the corn and the new wine and the oil unto
the treasuries.*

                    ❧ Nehemiah 13:11-12

*And I commanded the Levites that they should cleanse
themselves, and that they should come and keep the
gates, to sanctify the sabbath day. Remember me, O
my God, concerning this also, and spare me according
to the greatness of thy mercy.*

                    ❧ Nehemiah 13:22

Introduction

EVERY GREAT LEADER MUST ATTEND God's house; thus, we
entitle this chapter *church attendance.* In the thirteenth
chapter, Nehemiah re-instructs them regarding the house of God
and working on the Sabbath day. God's people need to be in
God's house. Nehemiah had been gone from Jerusalem, and he
came back to visit. Nehemiah saw *"some treading wine presses
on the sabbath, and bringing in sheaves, and lading asses; as
also wine, grapes, and figs" (Nehemiah 13:15).*

Sunday Must Be Sacred

In one of my Bibles, I have a small sticker that says, "Sunday
is a holy day, not a holiday." Sunday is not a travel day. You

must be at work on Monday morning, so you must travel on
Sunday. You ought to reverse that and say that you need to travel
on Saturday so you can get to God's house on Sunday. Being in
God's house is more important than being at work on Monday. In
Exodus 20, we find the Ten Commandments. Notice the Fourth
Commandment:

> *Remember the sabbath day, to keep it holy. Six days
> shalt thou labour, and do all thy work: But the seventh
> day is the sabbath of the Lord thy God: in it thou shalt
> not do any work, thou, nor thy son, nor thy daughter,
> thy manservant, nor thy maidservant, nor thy cattle,
> nor thy stranger that is within thy gates: For in six
> days the Lord made heaven and earth, the sea, and all
> that in them is, and rested the seventh day: wherefore
> the Lord blessed the sabbath day, and hallowed it.*
>
> ᴄᴅ Exodus 20:8-11

I realize this commandment is found in the Old Testament;
however, the Bible says that Jesus Christ did not come to destroy
the Law but to fulfill the Law. You should not throw away the
Old Testament just because of Calvary. The Sabbath of the Old
Testament was on the seventh day of the week, Saturday. In the
New Testament, the day set apart is the first day of the week instead
of the Sabbath. The Bible says,

> *In the end of the sabbath, as it began to dawn toward
> the first day of the week, came Mary Magdalene and
> the other Mary to see the sepulchre. And, behold, there
> was a great earthquake: for the angel of the Lord
> descended from heaven, and came and rolled back the
> stone from the door, and sat upon it. His countenance
> was like lightning, and his raiment white as snow: And
> for fear of him the keepers did shake, and became as
> dead men. And the angel answered and said unto the
> women, Fear not ye: for I know that ye seek Jesus,
> which was crucified. He is not here: for he is risen,
> as he said. Come, see the place where the Lord lay.*
>
> ᴄᴅ Matthew 28:1-6

The emphasis on the first day of the week is seen again in the book of Acts:

> *And upon the first day of the week, when the disciples came together to break bread, Paul preached unto them, ready to depart on the morrow; and continued his speech until midnight.*
>
> ∽ Acts 20:7

> *Now concerning the collection for the saints, as I have given order to the churches of Galatia, even so do ye. Upon the first day of the week let every one of you lay by him in store, as God hath prospered him, that there be no gatherings when I come.*
>
> ∽ I Corinthians 16:1-2

There needs to be a day that is sacred in this country and with God's people as well. I can remember vividly when stores were closed on Sunday. I can remember when gas stations were closed on Sunday. After that, I can remember about the date when Sears, Montgomery Ward, and other stores decided they were going to try to stay open on Sundays from 1:00 to 5:00.

> *There dwelt men of Tyre also therein, which brought fish, and all manner of ware, and sold on the sabbath unto the children of Judah, and in Jerusalem. Then I contended with the nobles of Judah, and said unto them, What evil thing is this that ye do, and profane the sabbath day? Did not your fathers thus, and did not our God bring all this evil upon us, and upon this city? yet ye bring more wrath upon Israel by profaning the sabbath. And it came to pass, that when the gates of Jerusalem began to be dark before the sabbath, I commanded that the gates should be shut, and charged that they should not be opened till after the sabbath: and some of my servants set I at the gates, that there should no burden be brought in on the sabbath day. So the merchants and sellers of all kind of ware lodged without Jerusalem once or twice. Then I testified against them, and said unto them, Why lodge ye about*

the wall? if ye do so again, I will lay hands on you.
From that time forth came they no more on the sabbath.
   ∾ Nehemiah 13:16-21

Nehemiah contended and testified against the people, and then he contended with the nobles, that is, with the presidents, leaders, and governmental officials of Judah. He told his servants that the gates were not going to be opened on the Sabbath day.

First of all, Nehemiah went to the general public. Secondly, he went to the rulers. Thirdly, he testified against those people selling and asked them why they lodged about the wall. He said, *"If ye do so again, I will lay hands on you"* (Nehemiah 13:21). I like Nehemiah. Nehemiah watched them sit there, and told them not to do this. For the last two weeks, he saw them sitting there. Once or twice he saw them do this. He closed the gates on the night before the Sabbath when it was getting dark. He stationed his guards there. He told the guards not to let anybody come in to buy or sell. The last couple of times he saw the men sitting by the gate ready to open up their wares and sell them. He had had it! If they tried to sell, he was going to lay his hands on them.

You may think that's not very Christian. It sounds Christian to me. Nehemiah was protecting the Sabbath. By the way, from that time forward they came no more on the Sabbath.

*I commanded the Levites that they should cleanse themselves, and that they should come and keep the gates, **to sanctify the sabbath day.***
   ∾ Nehemiah 13:22

A Place Must Be Sacred

The church, not some para-church organization, is the pillar and the ground of truth.

But if I tarry long, that thou mayest know how thou oughtest to behave thyself in the house of God, which is the church of the living God, the pillar and ground of the truth.
   ∾ I Timothy 3:15

The word *pillar* simply means a column that supports the weight of the structure, the weight of the building. The Bible says the church is the pillar—the support and strength—and the ground of the truth. The church is attached to Jesus Christ, and He is the ground of truth. Matthew 16:18 says, *"upon this rock I will build my church."* Organizations need to be built upon a rock. The rock is the ground. The ground is Jesus Christ, *"For other foundation can no man lay than that is laid, which is Jesus Christ"* (I Corinthians 3:11).

We should not go out and just build some little organization. There is no authority for that organization. There is no pastor. In His plan, God laid out what a pastor is; and his job is to oversee, to be a president over something. He is to be a preacher; he is to be a teacher; he is to be a shepherd. Then God gave deacons to help the pastor care for the flock. I do not find para-church organizations in the Bible. The church is vitally important in the life of every leader.

The church is important to godly leaders. Is it important to you?

CHAPTER 23

SEPARATION

*On that day they read in the book of Moses in the
audience of the people; and therein was found written,
that the Ammonite and the Moabite should not come
into the congregation of God for ever; Because they
met not the children of Israel with bread and with water,
but hired Balaam against them, that he should curse
them: howbeit our God turned the curse into a blessing.
Now it came to pass, when they had heard the law, that
they separated from Israel all the mixed multitude.*

          ஃ Nehemiah 13:1-3

Introduction

IN THIS CHAPTER, WE STUDY a leadership quality called
separation. Nehemiah 13:5 describes a great chamber that
Eliashib had prepared in the Temple for Tobiah the Ammonite,
the enemy of God's people. The Bible describes the previous use
of this apartment:

*Aforetime they laid the meat offerings, the frankincense,
and the vessels, and the tithes of the corn, the new wine,
and the oil, which was commanded to be given to the
Levites, and the singers, and the porters; and the
offerings of the priests.*

          ஃ Nehemiah 13:6

The tithes and financial gifts the people brought to the house of
God were kept in this chamber. The porters, the singers, and the
priests were paid from these gifts. God's people stopped tithing;

thus, they could not pay God's servants. They had to cut down on Temple worship, and they moved a wicked man who knew not the Lord into the room which previously stored the offerings of God's people.

Many of the great old fundamental churches of yesteryear, Methodist, Presbyterian, and Baptist churches that at one time preached the Word of God, often had a chamber built for missionaries, a preacher's apartment; and they had prayer rooms. Now, many of those rooms have Bingo parties in them. Many buildings that were once used as preaching stations are now an abomination. The chamber described in Nehemiah 13 was at one time a place where they have given offerings, but now they had moved in Tobiah.

> *But in all this time was not I at Jerusalem: for in the two and thirtieth year of Artaxerxes king of Babylon came I unto the king, and after certain days obtained I leave of the king: And I came to Jerusalem, and understood of the evil that Eliashib did for Tobiah, in preparing him a chamber in the courts of the house of God. And it grieved me sore: therefore I cast forth all the household stuff of Tobiah out of the chamber.*
>   ஓ Nehemiah 13:6-8

Nehemiah had gone back to check on his other work. Upon returning to Jerusalem, he understood the evil that had occurred. It was evil to move Tobiah into the house of God. The Bible calls it evil to move in modernism, to water down the gospel, and to lower standards. I love the story of Nehemiah evicting Tobiah. He did not call a committee meeting. He did not say, "Let's get together on this thing. Let me meet with all the ladies of the church first and see what they want to do; then I'll meet with the men." He just threw the man out.

The Practice of Separation

Just as Nehemiah threw out Tobiah, there are some things that we ought to throw out of our lives.

Be ye not unequally yoked together with unbelievers:

for what fellowship hath righteousness with unrighteousness? and what communion hath light with darkness? And what concord hath Christ with Belial? or what part hath he that believeth with an infidel? And what agreement hath the temple of God with idols? For ye are the temple of the living God; as God hath said, I will dwell in them, and walk in them; and I will be their God, and they shall be my people. Wherefore come out from among them, and be ye separate.

         II Corinthians 6:14-17

God says there must be separation from false religions. There needs to be a separation. God's people have always been separate. We should not be joining Tobiah to God's people.

God says Christians must be separated from unsaved people in choosing marriage partners. Christians are commanded not to be unequally yoked together with unbelievers. If a saved lady marries an unsaved man, she has violated the Word of God.

God says there must be separation in our appearance.

Doth not even nature itself teach you, that, if a man have long hair, it is a shame unto him? But if a woman have long hair, it is a glory to her: for her hair is given her for a covering.

         I Corinthians 11:14-15

God says there needs to be a difference in hairstyles between men and women.

The woman shall not wear that which pertaineth unto a man, neither shall a man put on a woman's garment: for all that do so are abomination unto the LORD thy God.

         Deuteronomy 22:5

That is strong language. Ladies, dress like ladies; men, dress like men. There needs to be a difference between the appearance of men and ladies.

Great leaders practice separation. Do you?

CHAPTER 24

STEWARDSHIP

And I perceived that the portions of the Levites had not been given them: for the Levites and the singers, that did the work, were fled every one to his field. Then contended I with the rulers, and said, Why is the house of God forsaken? And I gathered them together, and set them in their place. Then brought all Judah the tithe of the corn and the new wine and the oil unto the treasuries. And I made treasurers over the treasuries, Shelemiah the priest, and Zadok the scribe, and of the Levites, Pedaiah: and next to them was Hanan the son of Zaccur, the son of Mattaniah: for they were counted faithful, and their office was to distribute unto their brethren.

~ Nehemiah 13:10-13

Introduction

THIS CHAPTER DEALS WITH the subject of ***stewardship.*** Leaders must constantly remember the Biblical principles of stewardship. Whether you are leading a home, a business, or a church, you be a faithful steward if you expect God's blessings. Leadership without stewardship is improper leadership.

Money Problems

The Levites were those who were serving God and serving the people of God inside the Temple, and Nehemiah found that they had not been paid, *"For the Levites and the singers, that did the work, were fled every one to his field"* (Nehemiah 13:10). The Levites and the singers were not to be in the fields working; they were to be serving at the house of God. Nehemiah discovered that they had to leave the house of God and go back to the fields to work with their hands because God's people were no longer tithing. It is an amazing thing what many churches cannot do because God's people rebel against stewardship. Nehemiah asked, *"Why is the house of God forsaken?"* (Nehemiah 13:11). The house of God was forsaken because God's people refused to pay tithes. Nehemiah made *"treasurers over the treasuries"* (Nehemiah 13:13) because they were having money problems.

The beginning of the problem is described in the Bible:

> *And before this, Eliashib the priest, having the oversight of the chamber of the house of our God, was allied unto Tobiah: And he had prepared for him a great chamber, where aforetime they laid the meat offerings, the frankincense, and the vessels, and the tithes of the corn, the new wine, and the oil, which was commanded to be given to the Levites, and the singers, and the porters; and the offerings of the priests.*
>   ᴄᴀ Nehemiah 13:4-5

Though Tobiah was an enemy of God, they thought because their church was struggling a little bit, and things were not going too well that they should close down that big room, the section of the temple that they used to bring their tithes and their offerings and all of their money into, and not have it any more. They could rent it out to Tobiah. They could move him in, and make some money from him.

Money Promises
And the rest of the people, the priests, the Levites, the porters, the singers, the Nethinims, and all they that had separated themselves from the people of the lands unto the law of God, their wives, their sons, and their daughters, every one having knowledge, and having understanding; They clave to their brethren, their

nobles, and entered into a curse, and into an oath, to walk in God's law, which was given by Moses the servant of God, and to observe and do all the commandments of the LORD our Lord, and his judgments and his statutes; And that we would not give our daughters unto the people of the land, nor take their daughters for our sons: And if the people of the land bring ware or any victuals on the sabbath day to sell, that we would not buy it of them on the sabbath, or on the holy day: and that we would leave the seventh year, and the exaction of every debt.

                                 ✑ Nehemiah 10:28-31

In verse 31 they made a commitment to God that they would not buy or sell on the Sabbath day or on a holy day, and that they would not collect debts in the seventh year. They made ordinances to bring the firstfruits of their ground and the firstfruits of their trees year by year into the house of the Lord (Nehemiah 10:35). They agreed that to bring the firstborn of their sons and their cattle, as it is written in the Law; and they said they would also bring in the firstlings of their herds to the house of their God.

And that we should bring the firstfruits of our dough, and our offerings, and the fruit of all manner of trees, of wine and of oil, unto the priests, to the chambers of the house of our God; and the tithes of our ground unto the Levites, that the same Levites might have the tithes in all the cities of our tillage.

                                  ✑ Nehemiah 10:37

They were making God a promise. They were saying, "Our children belong to God, our cattle belong to God, our corn, our oil, our wine, and our trees belong to God. The firstfruits of everything we have belongs to God." Just as Proverbs 3:9 says, *"Honour the LORD with thy substance, and with the firstfruits of all thine increase,"* they had promised to give God their firstfruits. Their vow is recorded in the Bible:

For the children of Israel and the children of Levi shall bring the offering of the corn, of the new wine, and the oil, unto the chambers, where are the vessels of the sanctuary, and the priests that minister, and the porters, and the singers: and we will not forsake the house of our God.

                       ᕽᗆ Nehemiah 10:39

They had made commitments. They had said they would bring their firstfruits; they would bring their firstborn; they would bring everything to God. They were going to bring their offerings to a chamber in the house of God. They would bring it to the Levites and the priests and the Levites and priests would take care of it. They had said, *"We will not forsake the house of our God"* (Nehemiah 10:39).

They had forsaken the house of God when they stopped tithing. You will forsake the house of God when you do not tithe. I have yet to see people leave the house of God who tithe faithfully week after week, month after month, and year after year. When the devil gets into your pocketbook, it will be reflected in your church attendance. No matter how holy a person may look, how religiously he may speak, how influential he may be, what he may say about how great his pastor is, or how he loves his church, when a person has left the house of God, his tithing records, if you could see them, would demonstrate that he had not been tithing.

Money Privileges

And at that time were some appointed over the chambers for the treasures, for the offerings, for the firstfruits, and for the tithes, to gather into them out of the fields of the cities the portions of the law for the priests and Levites: for Judah rejoiced for the priests and for the Levites that waited.

                       ᕽᗆ Nehemiah 12:44

They said they were going to take part in tithing. They were going to involve themselves in tithing. They were going to set up a chamber, and bring the firstfruits of the tithe from all these cities to the house of God.

*Insomuch that we desired Titus, that as he had begun, so he would also finish in you the **same grace also**. Therefore, as ye abound in every thing, in faith, and utterance, and knowledge, and in all diligence, and in your love to us, see that ye abound in this grace also.*

                     ❧ II Corinthians 8:6-7

Chapters 8 and 9 of II Corinthians speak about giving. Giving is a grace. Grace means unmerited favor or unmerited privilege. We do not deserve the favor of God allowing us to have a part in stewardship; but God let us in on it and gave us the privilege of giving. The churches of Macedonia are given this touching tribute:

How that in a great trial of affliction the abundance of their joy and their deep poverty abounded unto the riches of their liberality.

                     ❧ II Corinthians 8:2

How to Give
1. *Give liberally.*

2. *Give willingly.*

For to their power, I bear record, yea, and beyond their power they were willing of themselves.

                     ❧ II Corinthians 8:3

3. *Give with equality.* There should be a fairness.

For I mean not that other men be eased, and ye burdened:

                     ❧ II Corinthians 8:13

4. *Give zealously!*

*For as touching the ministering to the saints, it is superfluous for me to write to you: For I know the forwardness of your mind, for which I boast of you to them of Macedonia, that Achaia was ready a year ago; and your **zeal** hath provoked very many.*

                     ❧ II Corinthians 9:1-2

Paul said he was bragging about their church. We are to give zealously. That means we are to be red-hot about giving; that we are to give with fervor.

5. *Give bountifully.*

> *But this I say, He which soweth sparingly shall reap also sparingly; and he which soweth bountifully shall reap also bountifully.*
>
>   II Corinthians 9:6

6. *Give purposely.* To give purposely means to premeditate about your giving. We ought to pray over our giving.

> *Every man according as he purposeth in his heart, so let him give; not grudgingly, or of necessity: for God loveth a cheerful giver.*
>
>   II Corinthians 9:7

7. *Give ungrudgingly.* Do not give grudgingly. Instead of giving grudgingly, give happily and be thankful you get to do it.

8. *Give cheerfully.*

9. *Give sacrificially.*

> *How that in a great trial of affliction the abundance of their joy and their deep poverty abounded unto the riches of their liberality.*
>
>   II Corinthians 8:2

Great leaders practice godly stewardship. Do you?

CHAPTER 25

DECISIONS

And I came to Jerusalem, and understood of the evil that Eliashib did for Tobiah, in preparing him a chamber in the courts of the house of God. And it grieved me sore: therefore I cast forth all the household stuff of Tobiah out of the chamber. Then I commanded, and they cleansed the chambers.

                                   ❧ Nehemiah 13:7-9

Introduction

THIS CHAPTER DEALS WITH THE FACT that leaders must learn to make *decisions.* When Nehemiah returned to Jerusalem, he had to make many decisions. Notice especially all the personal pronouns he uses:

I commanded, and they cleansed the chambers.

                                   ❧ Nehemiah 13:9

I perceived that the portions of the Levites had not been given them.

                               ❧ Nehemiah 13:10

I made treasurers over the treasuries.

                               ❧ Nehemiah 13:13

I testified against them.

                               ❧ Nehemiah 13:15

I contended with the nobles of Judah.

                               ❧Nehemiah 13:17

I commanded that the gates should be shut.
 Nehemiah 13:19

I testified against them.
 Nehemiah 13:21

If ye do so again, I will lay hands on you.
 Nehemiah 13:21

I commanded the Levites.
 Nehemiah 13:22

I contended with them, and cursed them, and smote certain of them, and plucked off their hair.
 Nehemiah 13:25

I chased him from me.
 Nehemiah 13:28

Nehemiah came to the city, and he made some decisions!

Seven Ingredients in Making Decisions

Listed below are several ingredients that I have used through the years in making decisions. As we prepare to look at these important ingredients, I must first remind you, however, that decisions are not based on emotions, convenience, money, the flesh, or hurt feelings.

1. Base your decisions on faith. Faith is a complete trust and confidence in God alone. The Bible tells us in Hebrews 11:1, *"Now faith is the substance of things hoped for, the evidence of things not seen."* Romans 14:23 tells us that *"whatsoever is not of faith is sin."* Hebrews 11:6 states, *"But without faith it is impossible to please him: for he that cometh to God must believe that he is, and that he is a rewarder of them that diligently seek him."* Habakkuk 2:4, Romans 1:17, Galatians 3:11, and Hebrews 10:38 all say, *"The just shall live by faith."* A godly decision must be based on faith.

2. Base your decisions on the Bible. For example, are you making a decision to handle booze? What does the Bible say on this matter? Are you violating some Bible principle? The Bible tells us not to look upon it and not to touch it. We are not to give it to our neighbor. Therefore, the decision has already been made in the Bible. Perhaps you are making a decision to date an unsaved person. The decision has already been made. You are not to yoke yourself with unbelievers.

3. Base your decisions on godly counsel. Proverbs 11:14 says, *"Where no counsel is, the people fall: but in the multitude of counsellors there is safety."* Proverbs 15:22 states, *"Without counsel purposes are disappointed: but in the multitude of counsellors they are established."* Proverbs 24:6 says, *"For by wise counsel thou shalt make thy war: and in multitude of counsellors there is safety."* Certainly there ought to be counselors for various areas of your life who give you direction when important decisions need to be made.

4. Base your decisions on the will of God. Romans 12:1-2 says, *"I beseech you therefore, brethren, by the mercies of God, that ye present your bodies a living sacrifice, holy, acceptable unto God, which is your reasonable service. And be not conformed to this world: but be ye transformed by the renewing of your mind, that ye may prove what is that good, and acceptable, and perfect, will of God."* Obedient people understand God's will. Do not expect God to reveal more of His will when you refuse to obey the will He has already provided for you.

5. Base your decisions on patience. Psalm 27:14 says *"Wait on the LORD: be of good courage, and he shall strengthen thine heart: wait, I say, on the LORD."* Too many life-changing decisions are based on the immediate. Be patient and learn to wait.

6. Base your decisions on what is pleasing to the Lord. I Corinthians 10:31 says, *"Whether therefore ye eat, or drink, or whatsoever ye do, do all to the glory of God."* You should ask if your decision will bring glory to God.

7. Base your decisions on experience. Genesis 30:27 says, *"And Laban said unto him, I pray thee, if I have found favour in thine eyes, tarry: for I have learned by experience that the Lord hath blessed me for thy sake."* Laban had discovered that God had blessed him because of his son-in-law, Jacob. When you do not have experience in some area, learn from the experience of others. When you have traveled the road before and have experienced the answer to this question, you will want to base your decision on your previous experience.

Nehemiah was a man who was a leader. He was putting a wall around his city, and he was a decision maker. When people came to try to hurt the work, he made a decision to stay in the battle. He made a decision to have them build with one hand and fight with the other hand. He made a decision about who was going to be set up over the city. He made a decision on how the job was going to get finished and how he was going to divide the people. He made a decision on how many days it would take. He made a decision that the people were going to get back to worshipping God. He made a decision that everyone would get back to tithing. He made the decision that there would be no work on the Sabbath. Throughout the thirteen chapters of Nehemiah, we see a man who was making decisions. Learn to make decisions.

Great leaders make decisions. Do you?